£8.75

Ruling Passions

Ruling Passions

❧

Sex, Race and Empire

Anton Gill

BBC Books

This book is published to accompany the
television series entitled *Ruling Passions*
which was produced by Roger Bolton Productions Ltd
for the BBC.
Published by BBC Books,
a division of BBC Enterprises Limited,
Woodlands, 80 Wood Lane
London W12 0TT

First published 1995
© Roger Bolton Productions Ltd and Anton Gill 1995
ISBN 0 563 37091 2

The moral rights of the author have been asserted

Designed by Tim Higgins
Maps by Alec Herzer
Set in Linotype Aldus by
Goodfellow & Egan Phototypesetting Ltd, Cambridge
Printed and bound in Great Britain by
Richard Clays Ltd, St Ives plc
Jacket printed by Lawrence Allen Ltd, Weston-super-Mare

Contents

Acknowledgements 6

Picture Credits 7

Maps 8

Foreword 11

Author's Note 13

1 Forbidden Fruit 15

2 Sweet, Just, Boyish Masters 57

3 Black Peril 89

4 Paying the Price 121

5 Missionary Positions 143

6 Children of Empire 161

Bibliography 185

Index 187

Acknowledgements

It is impossible to mention everybody whose contribution made this work possible, but thanks are especially due to the following people:

Dr David Anderson, Roly Armour, Professor N. D. Atkinson, Arthur Azuedo, Dr and Mrs Keith Batten, Roger Bolton, Harry Bowen, Maria Brennan, Len Brooks, Deborah Browne, Christabel Butler, Dick Cashmore, Dr Ratnabali Chatterjee, Jane Chege, Mary Cheptothon, Rosalind Cliff, Josh Cohen, Brigadier Tom Collins, James Cooper, Rosemary Cross, Arthur Cubitt, Helen Wamare Dadet, Taramoni Dasi, Colonel and Mrs Guyan Dubey, Jane Elliot, Henrietta Fanshawe, Tony Frith, Terence Gavaghan, Marie Godfrey, Fatima Hassen, K. C. Henderson, Cyril Hooper, Jaspeth Jedari, Jane Kenyan, Dr Isaac Lamba, Michael Lannas, Professor Anthony Low, Iris MacFarlane, Atta Wambui and Elizafan Machaga, Mervyn and Elsie Maciel, Grace Mani, Betty Matthews, Rupert Mayne, Donal McKenna, Gladys Minwalla, Margaret Muboni, Kibe Muciiri, Kit Mullan, Jocelyn Murray, Marion Nasoor, Pran Nevill, Ben Ngumba, Jeremiah Nyaga, Howard O'Connor, Abdul Osman, Aisha Osman, Raphael Onions, Edna Pierce, Colonel Wallace Pryke, Professor Ray Roberts, Dr John Sarkies, Amanda Sealy, Lieutenant-Colonel Gautam Sharma, Frances Shebbeare, Yardonath Singh, Ian Smith, Harold Smith, Zakia Stanley, Douglas Stanton-Ife, Dorothy Steel, Merfyn Temple, Patson Travers, Jack Vlahakis, Bila Wachuka, Rebecca Wanjiku, Diana Wasborough, Alex West, Lann White, Margaret Wiarimu, William Williams, David Wilson, Sister Aurea Wintel and John Wreford-Smith.

Picture Credits

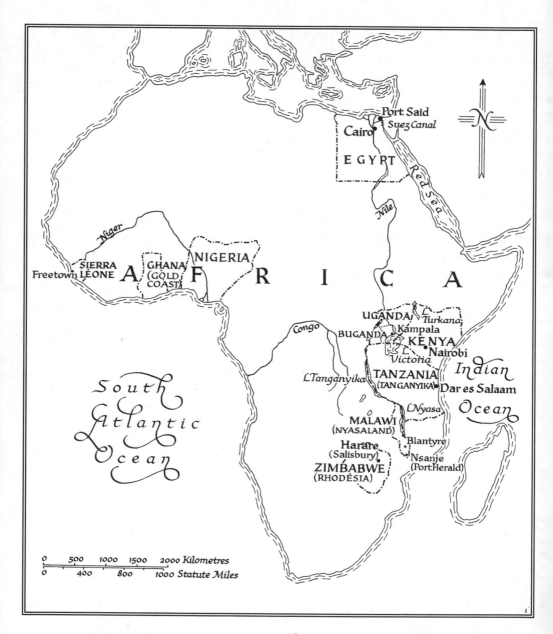

N

Port Said
Cairo
Suez Canal
EGYPT
Red Sea
Nile

Niger
SIERRA LEONE
Freetown
A
GHANA (GOLD COAST)
NIGERIA
F   R   I   C   A

Congo

UGANDA
Turkana
Kampala
BUGANDA
KENYA
L. Victoria
Nairobi
TANZANIA (TANGANYIKA)
Indian
Dar es Salaam
L. Tanganyika
L. Nyasa
Ocean
MALAWI (NYASALAND)
Harare (Salisbury)
Blantyre
ZIMBABWE (RHODESIA)
Nsanje (Port Herald)

South
Atlantic
Ocean

0   500   1000   1500   2000 Kilometres
0   400   800   1000 Statute Miles

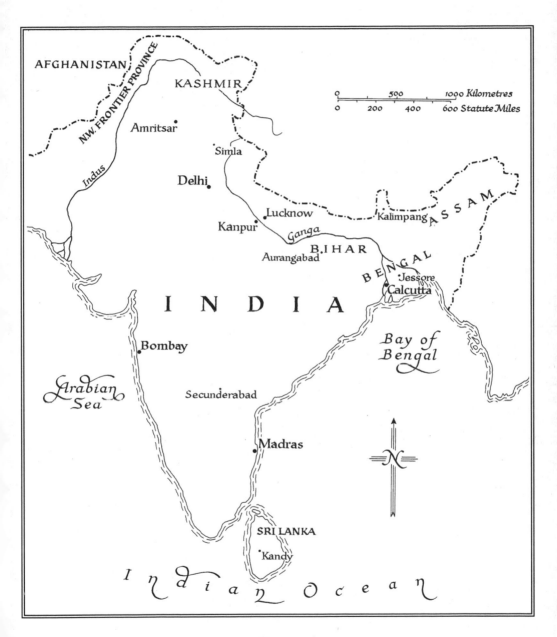

Foreword

The black and white Movietone image flickered in front of me. It looked very like my grandfather who, as Commissioner of Police, presided over the Bombay riots in the 1930s. I had last seen him more than thirty years ago in Kent. Here – if it was him – he was to be seen belabouring a demonstrator with his swagger-stick. Not a role I had ever imagined him playing, but not unlikely at that. Policemen have to keep the peace.

I am not alone. The British Empire seems to many to be ancient history, and yet there are probably millions of people in Britain today who have an intimate family connection with it, whether as rulers or ruled.

For most of us this past, a world of elephants and pageantry, brutality and dressing for dinner in the bush, is another country. Some time between Macmillan's Wind of Change and Callaghan's Winter of Discontent, and for many different reasons, British culture changed to such an extent that the eternal verities of only forty years ago are almost completely unintelligible.

One of those verities was the idea of the superiority of white people over black. Another was that the British Empire existed chiefly to bring peace, prosperity and development to precisely those black people. There are many old colonial hands for whom these propositions are still true – even if they may be unwilling to say so out loud. Equally, many British people today are descended from those who had to live under British rule overseas. Their understanding of the past is quite different.

Yet, oppressive or benevolent, principled or cynical, the Empire had a social dimension in which these opposites perforce became blurred. People met, loved, worked and played with each other as people, not always as representatives of a particular group or idea. By hearing the memories of these people, rather than looking at documents, we can have a slight inkling of how it felt to be part of this vast, ultimately amoral encounter. And, because it is at once a private and public thing, physical yet prone to fantasy, sex is a uniquely revealing avenue down which to travel. Sex is often the sticking point when push comes to shove in a conflict. Even when it was apparently at peace, the British Empire was in a permanent state of fermenting political and social conflict. Romeo and Juliet is a very old and often-told story, and it's usually a tragedy.

There will be many people for whom this book, and the television series with which it is linked, is missing the larger political or economic points. But in the end, Empire came down to individuals. Most of them had little choice about how they felt in any situation: fewer still had any real freedom of action, given the constraints of their background and the societies in which they found themselves. If we can understand the sources of their feelings, we can perhaps understand why the Empire took the shape it did, even perhaps understand our own position in the world today.

Indians and Africans who complain of the British obsession with Empire do so because they see it as an exercise in nostalgia. Although it was produced in Britain, *Ruling Passions* was deliberately not that, but nor is it definitive: no history is. There are many other stories still to be told about the British Empire, and they should be told, for it was an important moment in history.

As for me, the making of the series was a strange journey back through the mythology of my own family to understand perhaps why one great-great-uncle is reported as having 'gone to the bad' and ended his days in the Portuguese colony of Goa. Or why there are twelve Wilsons listed in the Bombay telephone directory. Of course, it's a very common name Wilson . . . .

DAVID WILSON
Series Producer

Author's Note

This book is based principally on the reminiscences and experiences of the colonizers rather than the colonized because it is concerned with the social constraint (and sometimes the liberation from it) of the British servants of Empire as they worked in its far-flung corners and came into contact with peoples who had very few of their sexual inhibitions. Because of the nature of society at the time, the relationships described are mainly between male colonizers and female locals, though behind that bald statement lie many gradations. No single history of sex and the Empire could possibly cover every aspect of its subject without risking superficiality or inordinate length. Readers who want to start exploring further should look at the list of books which follows this account.

The following explanations may also be of some help:

INDIA

The world *bibi* will occur from time to time during this narrative. It means 'lady' in Hindi, but it came to have the sense in colonial usage of 'native mistress'. An *ayah* is a children's nurse or nanny. A *syce* is a groom. *Mofussil* means 'out in the sticks' – remote.

In contemporary usage, 'Anglo-Indian' refers to a person of mixed British and Indian blood (formerly the term 'Eurasian' was used).

The spelling of the names of certain towns and areas in India has changed with time. Kanpur, for example, was spelt 'Cawnpore' at the time of the massacre there.

AFRICA

Several nations changed their names with independence, and former French West Africa, for example, has been replaced by a number of new countries along and beyond the Grain, Ivory, Gold and Slave Coasts – names that hold memories of the trades after which they were called. The COUNTRY which bore the name of the Gold Coast is now Ghana. Elsewhere in Africa, Nyasaland is now Malawi, Tanganyika is Tanzania, and Rhodesia is Zimbabwe. In former Nyasaland, the town then called Port Herald is now Nsanje; in Rhodesia, the capital, Salisbury, is now Harare.

An *askari* is a native policemen.

1

❦

Forbidden Fruit

And it's not for the sake of a ribbon'd coat,
Or the selfish hope of a season's fame,
But his captain's hand on his shoulder smote –
'Play up! Play up! and play the game.'

Vitai Lampada
Sir Henry Newbolt (1862 – 1938)

In the summer of 1897, the British celebrated, at great expense, the Diamond Jubilee of their seventy-eight-year-old Queen. Victoria had not always been popular, and her long withdrawal from public life following the death of her dearly beloved consort, Albert, had caused raised eyebrows and pursed lips at all levels of society a quarter of a century or so earlier. But the past couple of decades had seen a change in the grand old lady's fortunes. Her Golden Jubilee had confirmed her place in the public's heart, and twenty years prior to that, during the second administration of her Prime Minister and dear friend Benjamin Disraeli, she had become Empress of India.

The elevation was a master-stroke of public relations and the Queen herself was neither averse nor blind to its advantages. Indeed it was she who encouraged and pushed the somewhat harassed Prime Minister into putting the proposal before Parliament in the

15

form of a Bill for the Alteration of the Royal Title in 1876. It was angrily attacked by both Houses, but Disraeli defended it and saw it through with his usual urbanity and skill, and in doing so won his monarch's undying affection. She complemented her own promotion by making him a peer. According to Lytton Strachey in *Queen Victoria*:

> On the day of the Delhi Proclamation, the new Earl of Beaconsfield went to Windsor to dine with the new Empress of India. That night the Faery [as Disraeli called the Queen], usually so homely in her attire, appeared in a glittering panoply of enormous uncut jewels, which had been presented to her by the reigning Princes of her *Raj*. At the end of the meal the Prime Minister, breaking through the rules of etiquette, arose, and in a flowery oration proposed the health of the Queen-Empress. His audacity was well received, and his speech was rewarded by a smiling curtsey.

The Growth of Empire

Although India was always the jewel in the crown of Empire, it was never more than a part of a very great whole. The British Empire went back a long way, finding its origins in the discovery by the explorer John Cabot of Cape Breton Island in Nova Scotia in 1497 (he thought he had landed in Asia). But it was not until the emigration of the Pilgrim Fathers in 1620 that the Empire in North America and Canada began to take hold. Canada was wrested from the French in the mid-eighteenth century, and there were European rivals to contend with in the trading areas established in India and the Far East as well.

British involvement in India and Africa went back to the beginning of the seventeenth century, but while in Africa for at least two centuries the principal interest of the outsiders did not go further than the establishment of coastal forts for trade, in India the process was more intimate. The first English ambassador to the Indian court of Jehangir in Agra was Sir Thomas Roe, who was there from 1615 to 1618. By 1623, the British had established four 'factories' in the country – coastal depots at which goods bought at advantageous times and prices could be stored until the arrival of a merchant fleet to take them away. By 1647 twenty-three such depots had been built, and they formed the bases for settlements. A little more than twenty years later, Bombay was under British control, the peninsula having come to Charles II as part of the dowry of his Portuguese bride, Catharine of Braganza. This was by no means the earliest sizable British colony in India: Madras had been founded as the first English settlement in 1639. Towards the end of the seventeenth century British power increased as the new Mogul emperor, Shahjehan, the famous builder of the Taj Mahal, ousted the Portuguese from Bengal because they had refused to help him in his struggle against his father, Jehangir. The British replaced the Portuguese in Calcutta, which then became the capital of British India. By the mid-eighteenth century district governors were distributed throughout India representing the interests of 'John Company' – as the East India Company was familiarly known to its employees. With the decline of the Mogul Empire in India during the eighteenth century the East India Company developed a system of public administration to back up its financial and trade interests. By the late eighteenth century the Company had more or less ceased to be a trading concern, and become instead a 'corporation for the purpose of governing India under the direction of Parliament.' It lost its monopoly of commerce in 1813, and in 1833 it stopped being a business altogether. The Crown took over control of India from the Company in 1858, after a long period of transition.

There were, however, hiccups in relations with the locals and rival colonizers. In June 1756, in the course of a local uprising led by the Nawab of Bengal, Suraj-al-Daula, the British were obliged to flee Calcutta. Suraj rounded up those who couldn't or wouldn't go, and imprisoned them in the punishment cell of the fort, a room about 14 feet by 18, for the night. June is hot in Calcutta, and by morning only twenty-three – according to the British – of the original 146 prisoners remained alive. This was the famous Black Hole of Calcutta. The denouement was rather an anti-climax. Robert Clive, in charge of the East India Company Forces, retook Calcutta easily and reparations were demanded and received. The following year Suraj fought Clive's forces again at the Battle of Plassey. The French, who wanted to break British control in Bengal, supported Suraj politically. However, Suraj's generals mutinied and Clive was victorious.

Suraj became a close ally and even a friend of the British for the short time that remained to him after his defeat. Clive's victory established unquestioned British supremacy in Bengal, marking the end of a long aggressive campaign by the rival French colonizers to seize control there.

> ॐ The great colonial acquisitions in the southern hemisphere were only gained as Britain was on the point of losing her possessions in North America. Governor Arthur Phillip founded the first settlement in Australia at Sydney in 1788.
>
> The successful victory over Emperor Napoleon at the beginning of the nineteenth century brought with it acquisitions in the West Indies – Trinidad, Tobago and St Lucia – as well as, in the Indian Ocean, Mauritius and Ceylon.

In Africa, Britain gained control of the Cape, which in the days before the digging of the Suez Canal provided a welcome and necessary half-way house on the long voyage out to Bombay and Madras. Britain's first settlement in Africa had been James Island in the River Gambia in 1661, and there had existed trading posts and forts earlier still.

At the end of the eighteenth century the colonization of Africa got seriously under way, but the true era of expansion on the 'Dark Continent' came in the following century, when businessmen, explorers, missionaries and settlers – and sometimes, as in the case of David Livingstone, men who combined all four qualities – began to exploit the untapped resources that they found there. The late nineteenth century saw Britain gaining control of Egypt and the Sudan, though until the brutal and messy Second Boer War (1899 – 1902), the Afrikaners of South Africa maintained a stubborn independence, the reverberations of which are felt to this day.

Paradoxically the Empire did not reach the widest limit of its sway until long after it had passed its true peak. Queen Victoria's Empire made its first acquisition with the port of Aden in 1839; during the reign of her grandson George V the petty sheikdoms of the Hadramawt region along the southern edge of the Saudi Arabian peninsula were united under the Pax Britannica almost exactly a century later. But this was the last imperial moment.

It had been the greatest empire the world had ever known, both in size and, arguably, in quality. It excited harsh criticism: General Sir Thomas Munro, subsequently Governor of Madras, wrote in 1818: 'Foreign conquerors have treated the natives with violence, and often with great cruelty, but none has treated them with so much scorn as we.' It created its own myths: apart from early childhood, Kipling only spent seven years of his life in India, from the ages of seventeen until twenty-four, and he never returned once he had left. Neither Stanley nor Livingstone, Baden-Powell nor Rhodes, was quite the disinterested hero their first biographers presented to us. And yet for all the general exploitation and local injustice, the Empire worked. District Officers barely out of their teens were responsible for areas the size of large counties or small countries, with populations to match, and ran them successfully and alone, with a self-discipline born of an ingrained sense of duty and a specific kind of schooling. The entire European police force of India was about the same size as that of Britain, though India's population was at least four times that of the 'mother' country. The British soldiery never numbered more than 100 000; and yet with that small number, and without undue force, a vast subcontinent was successfully managed and developed. At its peak there were about

370 million people in the British Empire, and its gross product surpassed that of the rest of the world, including the United States, put together. Of those 370 million, only 50 million were white. Severity and even cruelty existed; racial distinctions were upheld and encouraged; snobbery and cupidity existed in generous amounts: nevertheless, Munro's judgment is severe.

Illusion and Reality

❦

In theory, and sometimes in practice, for Britons the Empire provided superb opportunities for adventure and self-improvement, both spiritually and materially. For most people, of course, adventure and profit were the prime motivations for leaving home. For some it was to escape hardship and unemployment. For many the reality fell far short of expectation: women especially, surrounded by unaccustomed servants and having nothing to do, trained to no interest and encouraged in none, would often succumb to boredom and the bottle. Intrigue was rife and so was scandal.

For everyone the challenges of a completely foreign environment – unfamiliar and often unappetizing food, heat, humidity, disease, large and unpleasant insects, squalid and teeming cities, and many others – were there to be overcome. In the early days, no one knew that mosquitoes had anything to do with malaria or bad water with cholera.

> ⋟ The main water supply for Calcutta was drawn from a large open pond called the Lal Diggee. One eighteenth-century correspondent observed of it, 'I saw a string of parria dogs without an ounce of hair on some of them and in the last stage of mange plunge in and refresh themselves very comfortably.' As for remedies during the same century Sir John Royds cured himself of some unexplained but near-fatal disease by drinking four bottles of claret a day until he recovered − as it turned out. Presumably his philosophy was kill or cure.

There were no modern light synthetic fabrics or 'breathable' materials in those early days: your best bet was muslin, or possibly silk if you were a woman. Men often wore European clothes and must have nearly died of discomfort. In addition to that for a long time, until Florence Nightingale pointed it out, the soldier's diet was − disastrously − exactly the same as if he'd been barracked at home. Among the common, though lesser, discomforts of the hot season was prickly heat (inflammation of the sweat-glands):

> . . . a sort of rash which breaks out on you, and, as its name implies, is prickly in its nature; I can only compare it to lying in a state of nudity on a horse-hair sofa, rather worn, and with the prickles of the horse-hair very much exposed, and with other horse-hair sofas all round, tucking you in. Sitting on thorns would be agreeable by comparison, the infliction in that case being local; now, not a square inch of your body but is

tingling and smarting with shooting pains, till you begin to
imagine that in your mouth you *must* have swallowed a packet
of needles, which now oppressed by heat are endeavouring to
make their escape from your interior, where they find themselves smothered in this hot weather.

Mrs Flora Annie Steel, co-author of the indispensable *Complete
Indian Housekeeper and Cook,* recommended sandalwood talcum as
a respite; but there was no remedy. The thing just had to be
endured.

In addition to these disadvantages must be added the sheer out-
of-touchness with home. Before the railway tracks were laid and the
telegraph wires strung, before the Suez Canal was dug and before
the long-distance steamer was developed, a posting to a far colony
was frequently lonely and often permanent. You never saw Britain
again, and if you did, it was often after a lifetime's absence during
which you had become a foreigner yourself, and the return to the
damp, grey little island which had so little to do with the rosy mem-
ory of home that you had nurtured for forty-odd years presented a
purgatory of problems with its vile weather, its claustrophobic
suburbs, its expensive cost of living and its lack of servants.

Alien Cultures

❧

Few colonials took an interest in or sought to understand the
native culture of the land they were posted to, though more
than might have been expected learnt the local language. Native culture was either a nuisance, faintly ridiculous, or threatening. At best
it was a source of amusement. It is true that in India, especially dur-

ing the eighteenth century when colonizers were more relaxed and less aloof in their attitudes, there existed a certain respect for and understanding of Hindu traditions. There was a common cultural root, after all, even if few were consciously aware of it, and Hindi was not such a difficult language to learn if you set your mind to it. As the East India Company moved into public administration there also grew up in India a sense of patriarchal responsibility.

In Africa the colonizers met not only an even more disparate cultural mix, but one which was – to their eyes – far less sophisticated, and certainly far more alien. Coupled to this was a more brutal approach to colonization. It started with trading in slaves, then gold and grain. It was followed by wholesale annexation of land for farming and mining, often marching hand-in-hand with evangelism. Just as it never seemed to occur to the secular colonizers that the land they took was not necessarily theirs by some kind of divine right, so the missionaries brought Christianity to the African aggressively, riding it roughshod over his beliefs, which few of them made the slightest effort to understand, and which virtually none respected. A borderline case was recorded by Livingstone himself, who at least tacitly cedes the argument to the pagan with whom he is in discussion, a witch doctor of the Bakwain tribe in Central Africa:

> WITCH DOCTOR: We both believe the very same thing. It is God that makes the rain, but I pray to him by means of these medicines.
> LIVINGSTONE: But we are distinctly told in the parting words of our Saviour that we can pray to God acceptably in His name alone, and not by means of medicines.

WITCH DOCTOR: Truly! But God told *us* differently. He made black men first, and He did not love us, as He did the white man. He made you beautiful, and He gave you clothing, and guns, and gunpowder . . . . God has given us one little thing, which you know nothing of. He has given us the knowledge of certain medicines by which we can make rain. We do not dispute those things which you possess, though we are ignorant of them. You ought not to despise our little knowledge, which you are ignorant of.

LIVINGSTONE: I don't despise what I am ignorant of; I only think you are mistaken in saying that you have medicines which can influence the rain at all.

WITCH DOCTOR: That's just the way people speak when they talk on a subject of which they have no knowledge.

LIVINGSTONE: God alone can command the clouds. Only try and wait patiently: God will give us rain without your medicines.

WITCH DOCTOR: Well, I always thought white men were wise until this morning. Whoever thought of making trial of starvation? Is death pleasant, then?

❧ A certain Baptist missionary couple spent thirty years in East Africa, retiring in 1970, and never learnt a word of any native tongue. They referred to all Africans as 'natives'. Their converts lived in a chicken wire compound, and were given T-shirts to wear and Coca-Cola to drink.

A Life Apart

❦

There was also the self-imposed problem of segregation. The traditional view is that this did not come about until the advent of large numbers of British women, especially in India, as travel from home to the subcontinent became quicker and easier. But in fact the British lived apart from the locals from the beginning. This was partly for reasons of health: one would find a neat British cantonment with houses in rows and manicured emerald lawns cheek-by-jowl with a swarming beehive of an Indian city. Partly it was a question of convenience. Most of all it was a matter of choice.

Indians and especially Anglo-Indians were employed in the Colonial Service throughout the eighteenth century, but as the East India Company acquired the status of a governing body, so local colleagues were increasingly discouraged and eventually squeezed out of all but the lowest cadre clerkships. The architect of this change was Lord Cornwallis, Governor-General of India from 1786–93, but he was essentially confirming a trend. By the 1790s the provinciality of colonial life in the early eighteenth century had given way to a sense of independence and freedom, and a sense too of their own identity among the ruling élite in the British capital of Calcutta. The English, who had at first sensibly adopted local costume, now wore European clothes. The middle-class élite knew that they enjoyed a higher standard of living than at home. They lived in some luxury and built themselves elegant, cool villas. They tried to close their minds to the heat and dust, the insects and the disease. They stuck together partly because of a natural tendency to do so and partly because the segregation was not one-sided. It would have meant defilement to a devout Hindu to eat with an Englishman, or even to touch him, while hardly any Muslim would drink wine (in public, at least), or risk eating non-halal meat (meat not slaughtered in the manner prescribed in the Koran). Indians of both local religions could be shocked by what they saw as unhygienic English eating habits – the English ate beef (offensive to Hindus) and pork (offensive to Muslims); they also ate (if doing so in native fashion) with the fingers of the left hand as well as the right and the former were used locally with water for cleaning the rectum after defecation. The amount of flesh exposed by English ladies was also shocking to Indians. Indian men were shocked, but not necessarily aroused – though this was the reputation they notoriously and undeservedly acquired.

Imperial Writings

❧

India and Africa, not to mention the other colonies, spawned libraries' worth of memoirs and travelogues. To a certain extent these give the lie to the assertion that the colonizers had no interest in their new environment; but works of the quality of Sir Richard Burton, Robert Orme, or J. W. Kaye are rare. It is significant that most of the books sympathetic to the alien culture were by women, who had some experience of being treated as second-class citizens themselves. Even so, against the impeccable attitudes of a Mary Hall or an Isabelle Eberhardt can be set the example of the American adventuress May French Sheldon, who was inclined to shoot first and ask questions later when it came to relations with the natives. Even quite liberal travellers like Mary Kingsley were daughters of their time in their fundamental belief in the superiority of whites, specifically English whites. Flora Shaw, the great Victorian traveller and journalist who married Lord Lugard and coined the name 'Nigeria' for the African country he was to govern, could write of 'this conception of an Empire which is to secure the ruling of the world by its finest race'; and Olive Schreiner, born in South Africa in 1855, could denounce Cecil Rhodes' profiteering, but didn't condemn Afrikaner exploitation of native Africans. She protested at the sexual exploitation of African women by the Boers, but still maintained the 'master-race' idea of ruling colonials.

On the whole the books written were of the 'Lone-European-versus-Savage-Elements' variety, whether those elements were human, other animal, or created by Nature in the form of roaring torrents or uncrossable deserts. Towards the end of the Empire, some fine novels were produced, in which colonial authors genuinely sought to identify with the problems and aspirations of the indigenous population of the land they lived in. As early as 1790 Sir William Jones was writing poetry about Hindu gods which shows real understanding of what they stand for. He discovered the linguistic link between Sanskrit (the ancient literary language of India) and Latin, German and Greek. This is counterbalanced, however, by popular doggerel in the style of well-known contemporary verse, such as the following anonymous offering, written a century later:

> *O grim and ghastly Mussulman,*
> *Why art thou wailing so?*
> *Is there a pain within thy brain,*
> *Or in thy little toe?*

The twilight shades are shutting fast
  The golden gates of day,
Then shut up, too, your hullabaloo –
  Or what's the matter, say?
The stern and sombre Mussulman,
  He heeded not my speech,
But raised again his howl of pain –
  A most unearthly screech!
'He dies!' – I thought, and forthwith rushed
  To aid the wretched man,
When, with a shout, he yell'd – 'Get out!
  I'm singing the Koran!'

Domestic Taboos and Foreign Escapes

❧

S et against the disadvantages of the colonial life, and outweighing them to a great degree, were the advantages. It was no bad thing to be born an Englishman of some education and standing between 1750 and 1850. Britannia ruled the waves and the pound sterling ruled the economies of the world. Vast swathes of distant continents were open to the Briton to explore and traverse as he pleased, and the attendant dangers, though they were there, were not often actually life-threatening and tended to be more inspiriting than alarming to someone who had received the sort of Spartan education doled out at public schools at the time. Another very obvious, even central, attraction was sex.

The great age of sexual repression in Britain came with the Victorian era, confirming a tendency set in motion by the Evangelical Revival of the late eighteenth century. Of all sins, sexual transgressions were the worst. Sex was something to be performed in the dark, if possible removing as few clothes as possible, an unpleasant prerequisite of producing children. At home in Britain a shadow hung over the whole activity. No one in the nineteenth century could openly express sentiments relating to it with the same jovial bluntness as eighteenth-century politician and wit John Wilkes had done:

> *Life can little else supply*
> *But a few good fucks and then we die.*

Abroad it was a different matter, though officially the British maintained a sexual aloofness alongside their social loftiness which was never shared by their Dutch, French, Portuguese or even German colonial rivals. In the big, bustling cities of Bombay, Calcutta and Madras it was much harder to maintain lines of distinction. In addition, many lower-class Europeans also lived there and they couldn't or wouldn't maintain standards of detachment, lacking the ingrained prejudice of their superiors. In Africa, an isolated District Officer might find himself in the centre of a local society which actually thought it bad for the man's health that he should be without a woman (a point of view incidentally shared by the French colonial administration). The British had got themselves into a position where they had made sex a taboo. But in the colonies it was different. One look at the erotic temple carvings at Khajuraho, or a dip into Richard Burton's translation of the *Kama Sutra* told you that.

They backed up their attitude with odd reflections. Because child marriage was common in India, the British got the idea that the

Indians were a more lascivious race. In Britain the age of consent for females had been raised, with the grudging consent of the House of Lords, from twelve to thirteen in 1875, but ten years later it went up to sixteen, the highest anywhere in the world. In the USA, for example, the age commonly fixed was ten. Male homosexuality was forbidden in any form whatsoever in Britain, and female homosexuality was too dreadful a concept even to mention, let alone pass laws on. In this atmosphere books like *The Arabian Nights* were thought more likely adversely to influence the undisciplined minds of Hindu and Moslem youth than their more fortunate British counterparts: 'Books that are innocuous to the comparatively pure and healthy morals of English boys may not be so to the more inflammable minds of Indian boys.' Never were the words 'pure' and 'purity' abused more in the pursuit of a dubious morality than in Victorian Britain, where social injustice and the exploitation of the poor were both infamous aspects of everyday life.

When Queen Victoria's reign was officially extended to India in 1858, administrative power there passed to the Crown, so the Governor-General's office became that of a Viceroy. With this distinction, especially following as it did the bloody and unpleasant episode of the Indian Mutiny the year before, came a even greater degree of aloofness than had existed before. But sexual aloofness, though desired and encouraged, was not adhered to. After all, this was the colonies, and one was off the leash. In any case, local attitudes to sex were so refreshingly different from the stifled *mores* of home. Although by the end of the nineteenth and beginning of the twentieth centuries Victorian sexual thinking had become so entrenched that according to Ronald Hyam in *Empire and Sexuality* 'whereas an eighteenth century soldier might take a copy of *Fanny Hill* [the erotic story of a prostitute's rise to respectability] with him to the French wars, a hundred years later it would be *Three Men in a Boat* which was found in the knapsack at Spion Kop [in the Boer War]', sexual feelings and desires did not go away, however fiercely men were encouraged to suppress them, and they accompanied colonists of all walks of life, from the most senior administrator to the humblest squatter, to the lands of opportunity.

At school in the 1940s, Tony Frith fed his desire for adventure with stories from *Boy's Own Paper*, *Masterman Ready*, and *Robinson Crusoe*. He studied forestry and ultimately the Colonial Office offered him a job in Sierra Leone. He set off to take up his appointment soon after the end of the Second World War on the former troopship *Highland Princess*. The passengers were crammed in eight to a cabin and included a large number of old Africa hands. During the ten-day voyage to Freetown he got his first introduction to what he might look forward to, apart from shouldering the White Man's Burden:

> When I first arrived in the cabin I was accosted by an old miner who came from the Gold Coast. He had me spotted as a green young man going out for the first time, and I suppose he was trying to shock me with his stories, using expressions that were completely alien to me, such as Mamipalava. 'What's that?' I asked him. 'It's what you do with those black mamas when you get out there, isn't it?' He used another term which I hadn't heard before, which was 'black tit'. I could guess what that was, of course, but I found it all rather shocking, and quite different from anything I'd expected from people who were working in the colonies.

1 Soon after his arrival in Bombay in 1920, Martin Sharp
fell in love with the daughter of the family with whom
he was lodging. The relationship was to lead to
much unhappiness for everyone concerned.

RIGHT
2 Tony Frith, whose schoolboy passion for adventure stories eventually led him to Sierra Leone in the 1940s. For a young Englishman the freedom to be found in Africa made a sharp contrast with life at home.

BELOW
3 Mahadaji Sindhia entertaining British officers to a nautch dance, Delhi, c. 1790. The nautch was an erotic dance of great refinement developed during the Mogul period.

Once installed at Freetown, however, and having been introduced to such delights as the rivulet where the native women, stripped to the waist, did their washing – 'the Europeans gave it the rather colourful name of Swinging Tit Creek' – the twenty-year-old forester soon became aware of the rather frightening possibilities. 'Freetown was a port, and being a port there was a great deal of prostitution. You could hardly walk the streets at that time without the girls accosting you from across the street. They would hiss at you to attract your attention.' But there was a serpent in this particular Eden, as in many other Edens, called vᴅ. 'You couldn't take any risks. And unless you were in the Forces, you couldn't get a condom. There were just none for sale.'

Prostitutes didn't provide the only temptation. There were the Bundu dancers too. These were girls barely into their teens whose traditional dances allowed them to show themselves off at their best, not least because they were topless. Frith remembers an unnerving experience when one day a group of Europeans from a saw-mill were having a drink at a Syrian store not far from Freetown and a group of Bundu dancers arrived in the square outside. 'The Syrian trader invited the Bundu dancers to come and entertain us. And they came up and sang a couple of songs just like a school choir. And then at a word from the lady who was in charge of them, they all split up and came and sat on our laps, and I had one on each lap; and it was a little difficult to know just what to do with your hands . . . . Then I discovered that they were completely covered with coconut oil . . . . ' Nothing more happened, and Frith believes that what did happen was no more than a bit of innocent fun, with perhaps a little teasing of the Europeans thrown in. The girls were certainly still too young to have been through their own sexual initiation ceremonies yet; but what elemental stuff for a young, traditionally brought up Englishman to be confronted with.

Eroticism: Real and Imagined

≈§§≈

Events like this were commonplace in the experience of British imperialists overseas, and the lascivious thoughts they inevitably prompted became a staple of the culture of the time. Rider Haggard's Victorian adventure novels were among the first to be filmed in the 1920s and early 1930s, and the film-makers didn't hesitate to portray his Africans as sexually powerful, active, and at once threatening and attractive. The pornographic films of the time also had an interest in the perilous excitement of dark skin. Indians were seen as dangerously rapacious, for example. The fact that in Africa women routinely went naked from the waist up suggested to the prurient European mind of the time a natural, uncivilized sexuality. White women, it was implied, had the same wild urges but had them properly under control – they were heavily clothed.

These attitudes went back as far as the first introduction of the different cultures to one another. In 1810 an African woman was brought to Britain and displayed for the delectation of paying English gentlemen. Anthropological interest often cloaked interest of a more basic kind, and in the 1820s one of the earliest pornographic novels, *The Lustful Turk*, graphically portrays the predicament of two English girls captured by a pirate and sold into the harem of the Dey of Algiers: 'My petitions, supplications and tears

34

were of no use. I was on the altar, and, butcher-like, he was determined to complete the sacrifice; indeed my cries seemed only to excite him to the finishing of my ruin . . . . '

The idea of the white woman in peril was taken very seriously, and was one of the most important indicators of the unconscious insecurity of the colonists. In fiction, however, it played salaciously upon pleasurable fears – the stuff of eroticism.

The eroticism of the East was real enough too, though far more delicate and refined than its portrayal in books like *The Lustful Turk*. European men certainly found Indian women attractive, especially if their first introduction was nautch dancers. The nautch is a traditional erotic dance of great refinement, developed during the Mogul period. (The Mogul Dynasty ruled India from 1526–1858.) Nautch was always a sophisticated, upper-class entertainment, and the art was handed down from mother to daughter. A dancer from Lucknow, Ano Parveen, remembers:

> The people we performed for were no ordinary people. They were big Nawabs and Rajahs. They gave us a lot. They presented us bags full of money. Even after giving the musicians and other people their shares, we were left with a lot. We invested most of the money in property. Those were the days of the Nawabs and Rajahs. We lived on what we got from them. At times we earned a lot from just one single show. At times they were so happy with us that they fixed lifelong salaries for us and our families. They made our life.

> ২ৡ A nautch dancer is fully clothed and sings and
> dances to the music provided for her. The erotic
> content is in the tone of her voice and in her facial
> expressions. To emphasize these, some dancers had
> the flesh at the corners of their eyes slit to make
> their eyes larger. The dance is slow, and the
> gestures intricate; the songs are about romantic
> yearning, and the art of the dancer is to address
> them personally to her audience. Audiences were
> always small – no more than ten people – and
> performances were accompanied with wine. The
> drinking was another element of the performance,
> as the wine made the spectator more susceptible.
> The performance was not done on a stage, but close
> to the audience, who sat or lounged on cushions.

The dancers themselves might also be courtesans, but not prostitutes. They would have a patron or protector who might keep them,
and they would remain faithful to him for the duration of the relationship. There were, however, prostitutes who passed themselves
off as nautch dancers and these devalued the art as time went on.
British men, too, ceased to attend nautch performances as the nineteenth century progressed and they retreated increasingly into their
own society. But by that time, relationships with Indian and Anglo-
Indian women had long been frowned on. Nautch continued to be
enjoyed by Indian patrons, however, especially in those areas not
under direct British rule. The Prince of Wales attended a nautch

dance in 1875 and again in 1890; but on that occasion it excited criticism and on a visit in 1905 there was no nautch dance for the new Prince.

In its heyday, though, nautch provided a convenient sexual bridge for the better-off Englishman to cross. Pran Nevill, a former Indian diplomat and chronicler of what he calls 'mercenary sex' throughout the world, has this comment: 'The fun-loving sahibs were naturally interested in sex also, and they picked up some nautch girls and kept them as mistresses. So that sex was there when they were enchanted with some nautch girl . . . . They found when they came here that the Indian way of looking at sex is entirely different. Everything was called perversion back home. But here it was not. In Hindu philosophy sex is something to be celebrated.' Prostitution was a perfectly respectable profession, and the *devadasis*, the girls attached to temples, would sell sex in order to earn revenue for the upkeep of the holy places.

In confronting such attitudes, allure and repulsion sometimes went hand in hand. In the less hidebound eighteenth century, allure had the upper hand, and it maintained its supremacy for many – perhaps one could say for most – as long as the British were in India. For some it was a simple proposition. Edward Sellon, a British Indian Army officer of the 1840s, had no embarrassment about the joys of the East: 'I now commenced a regular course of fucking with native women. They understand in perfection all the arts and wiles of love, are capable of gratifying any tastes, and in face and figure they are unsurpassed by any women in the world . . . . It is impossible to describe the enjoyment I have had in the arms of these syrens . . . .'

37

Science and Superiority

✺§§✺

Sellon was more than just a voluptuary. He was also a scholar, one of the new Victorian movement that took anthropology seriously. Many Victorian visitors to Africa and India saw native people as primitive savages, however, and set out to prove this scientifically with observations of African and Indian sexual practices. Of one aspect of Hinduism, Sellon wrote: 'The *Sacti* is personified by a naked girl to whom meat and wine are offered, and then distributed among the assistants. Here follows the chanting of the *Muntrus* and the sacred texts, and the performance of the *Mudra*, or gesticulations with the fingers. The whole terminates with orgies amongst the votaries of a very licentious description.'

But it was the physical characteristics of black peoples that were the key to the Victorian anthropologist's work. One of the leading lights in the nascent science was the great explorer and linguist, Richard Burton.

Burton was born in 1821, and after a time in India he lived a life of great adventure. He dressed as a Muslim Indian doctor and smuggled himself into the forbidden city of Mecca; he discovered Lake Tanganyika, and visited the Kingdom of Dahomey in West Africa. He also travelled widely in North and South America. Everywhere he went he took down detailed descriptions of the sexual customs of the peoples he visited, and he drew some bold conclusions:

> Debauched women prefer Negroes on account of the size of their parts. I measured one man in Somali-land, who, when

38

quiescent, numbered nearly six inches. This is a characteristic of the Negro race and of African animals; e.g. the horse; whereas the Arab, man and beast, is below the average of Europe . . . . Moreover these imposing parts do not increase proportionally during erection; consequently the 'deed of kind' takes a much longer time and adds greatly to the woman's enjoyment. In my time no honest Hindi Moslem would take his womenfolk to Zanzibar on account of the huge attractions and enormous temptations there and thereby offered to them . . . .

His observations are not wrong. The science of penis-measuring is called phalloplethysmography, and it has established that the black penis is indeed on average a *little* larger than the white. That the black man is sexually more potent than the white is a belief that has been held (by white men at least) since the fifteenth century, and the envy to which this has given rise may also account in part for the irrational but persistent fear for the virtue of white women in the colonies.

Burton's clinical manner was aimed at a particular group of interested people, the unembarrassed minds who attended with him the meetings of the Anthropological Society of London, which he had helped to establish precisely to publish accounts which would otherwise have been censored or suppressed. He called it 'a refuge of destitute Truth', which permitted 'a liberty of thought and a freedom of speech unknown to any other society in Great Britain.' The first article published by the Society was by Burton's co-founder James Hunt. In it, Hunt asserted that Negro cranial sutures closed earlier than those of white men, and that therefore their brains were smaller.

Burton died in 1890. Unforgivably but, in the context of her age, understandably, his wife burned his diaries. By the end of the century anthropologists, helped out by Darwin's idea of the survival of the fittest, were claiming that science showed that the white races were superior, not just because of their physical and mental make-up, but because their sexual *mores* were more 'civilized', derived as they were from Christian ideas of abstinence and monogamous marriage. Christian ethical and moral values as they related to sex were enforced by the various missionary societies and the sometimes closely associated Purity Movement.

Iris MacFarlane's family had been involved with the Raj for generations through the Army. By the time she arrived in India as a teenager in the 1930s, white supremacy and Christian rectitude were still very well entrenched:

> We had a priggish feeling about Indians. We were so self-right-eous. We were educated and Christian and clean and orderly; and they were just a sort of uneducated heap of humanity, really. We didn't understand their religion then, and we looked on them as idol worshippers some of whose rites were so horrid that we didn't like to look into them too much. We had such an innate sense of superiority that we simply regarded them as a poor, uneducated lot who hadn't seen the light, and we were very glad that they were like that because then they didn't threaten us in any way, because we had it all.

The scientific approach allowed people to contemplate sex in the raw without compromising Victorian social etiquette. At the same time, this disinterested approach reduced the native peoples under scrutiny to the status of a bug in a Petri dish – worth studying, but of infinitely less intrinsic value than the observer. This kind of anthropology overflowed into popular culture. Anthropological photographs, ostensibly taken for scientific reasons, took on the tone of the pin-up. Richard Burton chiefly became well known, not to say notorious, for his translation of the *Kama Sutra*.

Sex and Status

By the 1890s, the British encounter with the world outside Europe had created an expectation that sexual pleasure there could be had far more excitingly than in Europe, let alone than in the British Isles. But sexual extravagance abroad was not condoned because of distance, or forgiven because it was indulged in with peoples of other cultures and races. There were scandals, and great men were brought down by them as their sexual proclivities were exposed. In 1902 General Sir Hector Macdonald was appointed Commander-in-Chief, Ceylon, at the age of forty-nine. He was a distinguished soldier, a star both of the Battle of Omdurman and of the Boer Wars, a humble crofter's son who had risen from the ranks to the top, and revered now as a national hero in Scotland. He had married, at the age of thirty-one, a sixteen-year-old Scots girl by whom he'd had a son, but the marriage was not a success, and collapsed within a decade. Macdonald's main relationships were with boys and girls of school age, though these were limited to sentimental attachments at home. Disaster struck in 1903, when he was interrupted by a planter, *in flagrante delicto* with no fewer than four Sinhalese boys in a railway carriage at Kandy. The matter might have been hushed up, but it was decided to make an example of Macdonald. At first he denied the charges, but in the end he shot himself that same year.

His fate was viewed with sympathy by Sir Roger Casement, who had spent his life in the service of the anti-slavery movement, scoring significant victories against slavery both in the Belgian Congo and in Peru. But in the year that Macdonald died Casement started to write his 'black diaries', which by a miracle have survived. They reveal the hero of reform to have been an enthusiastic and energetic homosexual. Here is a diary entry from February 1910, written in Rio de Janeiro ('X' stands for sexual intercourse):

> Deep screw and to hilt X 'poquino'. Mario in Rio 8.5 x 6 inches 40$. Hospeclaria, Rua do Hospicio 3$ only FINE ROOM shut window lovely, young, 18 and glorious. Biggest since Lisbon July 1904 and as big. Perfectly huge. 'Nunca veio major.' Nunca.

Casement was not exposed during his lifetime – he was shot as a traitor by the British in 1916 for his part in the Irish Revolution – but the strain of concealing his true nature from a society which would immediately have condemned him to the outermost darkness was clearly something which destroyed this great man's personality. Italy and Holland had abolished homosexuality laws directed against consenting adults in private by the 1880s. But Britain had become a bastion of prudery with regard to sex.

If you were reasonably discreet – and you didn't even need to be that very much before the nineteenth century – and you weren't too prominent a figure, it was easy to find sexual action anywhere in the Empire. Marion Nasoor, a Kenyan born about 1920, worked as a housekeeper and nanny for various white families from her teens on, and recalls that 'there was a lot of sex between the employers and the employees'.

The first time it happened to her was when she and her male boss took his kids off on a day's safari, leaving the wife at home. The children were still very small, and the husband made love to her in their car. Marion herself didn't feel badly about it. All her friends were doing it, too, and generally a lot of pride attached to the relationships; the African woman considering that she belonged to the man: 'Men often had affairs with their *ayahs*, but they kept it a secret. They would take you to the movies with the kids and then you'd both surreptitiously steal away. Once you'd got the kids settled, you'd go back to the lodgings or to the motor car.'

The local men knew what was going on, but to be a white man's mistress gave the black woman status in their eyes. There were also presents – though these usually took the form of cash payments rather than clothes or jewellery because in such a case a white wife might notice the goods and put two and two together. But it wasn't always a question of straight sex as Marion recalls:

> The really important thing, the one thing they couldn't get – and please be discreet here – was that if you agreed that he could do it to you from behind he would even give you a ring – he would promise you the earth, and he would never let you go. That was the thing. To go in from the back. Man to woman or man to man. Even today that is true. Even today if a man wants employment from white people, he has to agree to be done from the back. Even now, even now, even men.

Mary Cheptothon also worked as a nanny in Kenya at that time:

White men were supposed never to tell lies, but they kept their relationships very secret. Even if you tried hard you could never discover the white man's secrets. Even when I was working for one I would never discover his secrets. But if you showed yourself to be trustworthy, he might take you into his confidence. For example, if I was working as an *ayah* and the man felt that he could rely on me, he might ask me to procure another *ayah* that he had his eye on. We might be out walking with the children, and the white man might see another *ayah* that he fancied. 'Is she good?' he would ask. I would say 'Yes', and he would ask me to arrange something, and I would agree. Why not? And I would even get on well with the man's wife – because he'd be confident that I wouldn't peach on him.

What made all this easy was the master-and-servant relationship between black and white which ran right through the Empire. Whatever their cultural and moral attitudes, black people in general were much poorer than their white rulers. One way in which they could improve their own situation materially was through the sale of sex. No shame was necessarily attached to this, either.

In Sierra Leone, forester Tony Frith was in the throes of a platonic love affair with a Euro-African artist when he was approached by Sonia:

She offered me my first actual sexual experience. I'd had none at all before I went out to West Africa. I was still only just twenty-one years old. Sonia was a nurse who worked in the local hospital, and she simply came round and knocked at the door of the cottage I was living in at that time in Freetown. I invited her in, and she said to me, 'You don't have a woman, do you?' And I said, 'No, no.' She said, 'Well, I would like to be your woman.' This was the first opportunity that I'd had. She

44

said, 'You don't have to worry about me, I'm a nurse; I know what to do.' She added that as nursing was poorly paid, she was looking for some extra money. Apparently she knew all about me, and she was fairly sure that I was completely innocent at the time. The steward boy or the cook would have told her anything she needed to know about me. She actually seemed quite pleased that she could offer me this service. I was a healthy young man, and a little bit of sex didn't seem to come amiss. I paid her about a pound every time she visited me.

The Africans had their own standards of sexual propriety, but to some extent this depended on class. Frith's platonic mistress was a class above Sonia, and better off materially; her ideas regarding a sexual relationship would have been a good deal more formal than the nurse's. But for Sonia it was simply a question of commercial opportunity. In the end, the young Frith was taken under the wing of an English couple.

There was one particular major and his wife who got to know me very well. They were a happily married couple, and so they always wanted to be matchmakers. 'We must find you one of the nursing sisters,' they told me. A new batch was expected to be arriving from England soon, and one of them, so I was told, would appeal to me. In the event she did, and we married. It never occurred to me then that the major and his wife had wanted to get me married just to keep me on the straight and narrow – but it might have been. Yes, it might have been.

Serious affairs of the heart – of the kind Tony Frith had with the artist – were frowned upon. The combination of power and racial arrogance made sex easy to come by for Europeans; but love was another matter.

45

> ❧ Even when relationships were not on a cash basis, the contempt which the majority of British people often had for other races meant that they often regarded them as fair sexual game, with no

Abuse and Abandonment

❧§❧

Edna Pierce was born in Rajasthan of an English mother and an Anglo-Indian father. She remembers how the British soldiers from the large cantonment barracks in Lucknow behaved towards her Anglo-Indian friends during the Second World War.

The men who were from good families were all right – they were very friendly with the Indians, but others were very rude and cruel. They would say very unkind things to the girls, but the girls would never take any heed of it – they were crazy about the soldiers and wouldn't listen to advice. Those girls went and married them – but they had civil marriages, not marriages that the Army recognized. That's why the soldiers left them in the lurch in the end. But even before that they used to abuse the girls, calling them black this and black that in front of everyone. Some of the girls weren't black at all – they had quite fair complexions, but that didn't stop the soldiers from insulting them, abusing them in Hindi, which can be a very dirty language.

I didn't expect Britishers to behave in that manner, especially to women. I remember that they used to pick girls up in the dance halls of the Hazrat Ganj in Lucknow, but they would manhandle them and molest them. I hated them for that. And at the end of it all, when they left, all the girls – some wives, some with babies – stood around to see them off, crying, 'Come back, Bill, come back,' and the men replied, 'Yes, Jane, we'll come back.' But they never did.

Some of the abandoned mothers got jobs at the Secretariat, but there was no official support whatever for these single-parent families for whom the British administration was indirectly responsible. Edna Pierce recalls that the few girls who were taken back to England fared no better: some even found that their husbands were already married, and attempted to pass their Anglo-Indian wife off to their English wife as a servant. This experience so affected one of Edna's friends that she went mad.

Gang-rape was not uncommon; but it was not only women who were subjected to violence. Rickshaw-drivers were frequently hired by soldiers to take them to and from either dances or the brothels. Often the soldiers would refuse to pay their fare, and if the driver raised any objection, the consequences could be dire: 'One night-time after a dance a poor rickshaw man took a soldier back to the barracks, and in the morning we saw him lying in his rickshaw, bleeding in a pool of blood. They'd cut off his private parts and put them in his mouth. We saw that with our own eyes – all of us were going to work, and we saw it.'

The Colour Thing

🦢

Almost all British people in India at the height of the Raj shied away from the possibility that sexual relationships could be carried on with the subject races on an equal basis, even if the 'natives' had some English blood. The rules in this respect applied especially to young English girls. Iris MacFarlane remembers vividly her feelings as a teenager sixty years ago:

> I really can't understand or explain it. It was just horror and nausea, and a sort of drawing physically away from anybody who was coloured. This was especially true of Anglo-Indians because they could be a threat in that they could infiltrate your world without your knowing it, unless you were very careful. So you had to learn all the little signs, which you had to learn when you went out. However fair their skins, there were always the little signs – the fingernails, and the ears, and the whites of the eyes, for example. I'm sorry to say that I do remember starting to watch out for these signs. I didn't always pick them up though. I remember that I went to a sort of short-hand typing course once and one of my fellow students was a very blonde, blue-eyed, pink-faced girl, and I thought, she's all right, so I took her home. But the first question my mother asked her was, 'What does your father do?' and she said, 'He's in the railways.' Well, that was it. Anybody in the railways was absolutely bound to be Anglo-Indian. So that was the end of her. She wasn't allowed back to the house again. And of course the same went for men. I was told who was within my marriage range and who wasn't. Anybody, however old or decrepit, bald or dull, was a possible husband, as long as he was white. But anybody with the slightest touch of colour wasn't.
>
> I don't quite know what we were afraid of. We weren't afraid of them attacking us – I don't ever remember any feeling of being physically afraid of them. But there were so many of them and so few of us.

Perhaps something was built into them. From her letters, it appears that Iris MacFarlane's great-grandmother, a Dartmouth girl who married and went out to India in the mid-nineteenth century, had the same horror of colour. In the letters, her great-grandmother, who spent seventeen uninterrupted years away from England and bore ten children in India, tells her eldest daughters never to let their Indian maidservants kiss them or even touch them, for fear of contracting some appalling but unspecified diseases. What could they have been? Were cholera and malaria associated with Indians rather than water and mosquitoes? Did the white men, who clearly had no inhibitions when it came to physical contact with the locals, encourage such prejudices to keep their women apart?

'You occasionally met Indians at dinner parties – very high-class Indians. I was allowed to go out with Maharajahs – there was something about their being very rich that overrode the colour thing,' recalls Iris MacFarlane. She also remembers being allowed to socialize with an Oxford-educated nephew of Jawaharlal Nehru and his wife, but the couple were only ever invited to tea on their own, never to a dinner party. 'I think some of the Indian Civil Service people were perhaps a little bit more relaxed about it. But we were an Army family – and the Army was still very much in a rut.'

Kit Mullan grew up in Nyasaland and the West Indies and then spent much of her adult life in Assam. She puts a slightly different point of view: 'We made lots of friends with Indians, but it didn't get any further. I mean to say, I don't think that if our sons and daughters had been anxious to marry each other, any of us would have been at all pleased. I mean, the prejudice was as much with them as it was with us.'

There could be other bonding factors that bridged the gap between colonial and local. One lady who spent her youth in Kenya recalls the blessing of a shared language: 'Swahili was a great welder together because we all had to learn it: Indian, up-country African, and European. We all had to make an equal effort to understand one another.' This did not mean that they automatically shared anything else, however. The same lady also came up against strong elements of African conservatism: 'To begin with it was difficult because they would not have their women educated. They would not let their women change. The idea was that if you educated a boy, well, you'd changed a man; but if you educated a woman, you'd changed a family; and if you'd changed that, you'd changed a tribe. And so they kept their women back for years and years, and it was really no good trying to force the pace.'

Iris MacFarlane's upbringing did not prevent her from finding individual Indians attractive: 'The most attractive man I've ever met in my life was a Bengali. If I'd been free I'd be sitting in Bangladesh now,' she laughs. 'The Bengalis were a charming, intelligent, artistic people, and he was just everything that I thought was perfect in a man. There was a sort of stuffiness about the British, whereas the educated Indians were very much more relaxed and usually much more interesting too.' Ultimately, she married a Scottish tea planter.

The kind of systematic prejudice passed on by generations of British imperial rule was reinforced by official attitudes according to which Indians were not allowed into the British clubs, or invited to the Viceroy's garden parties. The agony this segregation sometimes caused could be immense. One young Englishman, Martin Sharp, born in 1900, went to Bombay in 1924 to work for the large general trading company of Sassoon's. The predicament he soon found himself in there remained a secret for nearly seventy years, until his daughters looked at his letters home, and those diaries which he had not destroyed, after his death in 1987.

His first lodgings were in a 'chummery' – a house or flat where a group of bachelors lived and clubbed together to pay for food, drink and servants. Often only marriage would get a man out of his chummery, but Martin moved into a private family house as a paying guest. He soon became friendly with the children of the house, especially a daughter, Pauline, who was seventeen years old.

Martin enjoyed all the privileges of Raj life – he played squash and tennis, he swam, and hunted jackal on horseback; but at bottom he was a little insecure. It took him a while to get used to his new environment, and he was worried about how well he'd be regarded in his job. His diaries reveal pronounced views in favour of segregation, and upon that attitude his story depends.

Martin and Pauline began to go out together – at first simply as friends, but as timed passed he became aware that he was falling for her. One night, about three months after they had met, 'I was able to take Pauline after dinner to see the Kai Hawaiian musicians at the Excelsior. They were jolly good and we did enjoy it. A most unbelievable thing happened when we were saying goodnight at Pauline's bedroom door. We sort of fell into each other's arms and kissed, all without a word of warning or a second's reflection . . . . It was two hours before I could get to sleep.'

But all was not plain sailing. Martin's diary describes a number of misunderstandings and tiffs, though on the whole the romance flourished. Oddly, they seemed to be able to get away without having a chaperone, sometimes taking a taxi to the Malabar Hills and spending hours there entwined. Martin, a young man of strict principles, considered that he had already gone far enough to feel committed to Pauline for life, and he did genuinely love her. Their innocent love-making continued meanwhile – once, on the drawing-room sofa late at night, they kicked over a brass bowl noisily and woke the house, explaining their presence downstairs by saying that they'd gone to fetch glasses of water. One wonders how naïve Pauline's parents were.

Throughout all this, Martin had been trying to find out more about Pauline's background. She was a redhead and had been educated in England, though born – which was a disadvantage socially – in India. Her father worked for the telephone company. There were slight shadows: it transpired that Pauline's mother was half-Greek. An uncle had very dark skin – something which Martin attributed not unreasonably to the effects of malaria. When his time for leave in England came he got engaged to Pauline and left, determined to find a job there, so that he could bring her home and settle down. This venture failed and another uncle of hers whom he approached in London refused to meet him, brusquely informing him that he had nothing to do with the Indian branch of the family.

He returned to Bombay uneasy, but with his mind still fixed on marriage. He was no longer at Pauline's family home. Pauline had hinted at 'happy secrets' which would be revealed once they were married, but he was not reassured. The Secretary of the Bombay Gymkhana Club had told him not to bring Pauline there. As membership of the club was central to his social life, this was a severe blow. Pauline's family were not invited to Government House when the Viceroy paid a visit to Bombay. Still Martin could not face the suspicion that was beginning to grow in his mind.

In April 1925 Pauline's father told Martin that he thought it would be a good idea if he and Pauline married without any further delay. Martin's suspicions would not allow themselves to be ignored any longer. A month later, some members of the family were involved in 'irregularities' in Calcutta. This precipitated the crisis. Martin described it in a letter to his parents:

> It was clear to me that Pauline never had any real love for me, and was marrying me simply to be raised from Eurasian to European status at the expense of lowering me and probably losing me my job . . . . So last Saturday I 'phoned her father from the office and asked if I could call. I intended to ask them if my fears were correct and to judge from their manner of answering what was the truth of the situation. I expected the interview to last half-an-hour; it lasted six minutes. I simply said, 'I think Pauline and the two of you have been deceiving me all along, and I want to thrash the thing out. First of all, is there any Eurasian blood in you?' There was a pause of several seconds, and therefore I knew they were Eurasians, for if you put that question to an Englishman he would knock you down. I felt as if the end of my uncertainty had come and with it the end of my happiness. Then her father flared into a rage, saying he declined to discuss with me whether there was black, white, yellow or any other blood in him, and that he was insulted, and that Pauline was to give me back my ring at once . . . . He then ordered me out of the house, but showed no signs of immediate violence, and I had for one second a fearful sensation that perhaps I was wrong. I turned to Pauline and said, 'Am I mistaken? Are you pure white?' She wouldn't answer but looked away, and as I stepped to the door, she said, 'You have insulted the whole family' . . . . You know what I thought of Pauline.

> Can you wonder I've been unhappy for the past year, can you imagine how I feel now? It's not nearly so bad in the daytime, but at night here in the loneliness of my rooms, when the dictates of common sense fall before the cause of sentiment, it is awful. I can't sleep and I can't digest anything. It's 5.30 as I write this and the morning greyness is appearing in the sky.

Soon afterwards, he returned to England and married there. Pauline and Martin never met again. His daughter Rosalind says, 'I think his greatest worry was that he might have made a mistake, and there were two reasons why he might have done so: he might have made a mistake because she was not of Indian blood; but he might have made a mistake in not going ahead with the marriage anyway.' It is interesting that if he had married Pauline, who did not *look* Indian, in England, the fact that she was Anglo-Indian might not have mattered a fraction as much as it did in India.

Ignorance and Fear

◦§§◦

Dr David Anderson of the School of African and Oriental Studies in London believes that the Black Peril idea found among colonizers has its roots in the settlers' own sense of isolation. Settlers 'make their own society, and that society is made by defining itself as being different from those people of other races around it. So that there is a sense of anxiety in the very making of a settler society.' The idea that local people might be diseased was also a contributor to anxiety. British colonial policy regarding public health in Africa was informed by ideas of sanitation from the turn of this century onward. Africans were seen essentially as pollutants of

Europeans: they carried diseases to which Europeans were not immune and this led to those notions of segregation on grounds of health which have already been mentioned. Venereal disease was an especially nasty spectre – the African disease yaws was difficult to distinguish in its symptoms from syphilis. Ignorance was compounded when, as happened quite often, British colonials set off with only the faintest idea even of where they were going. Kit Mullan recalls her father's first appointment in 1901:

> He always said that it was a toss up as to whether he got a job as a magistrate in Nyasaland or a lecturer in English at Christchurch University in New Zealand. The Nyasaland job came through the letterbox first, and he was keen to be off. He went to the Colonial Office and asked them how he could get there, as he was rather vague about where it was. And they took out some maps and scratched their heads and said, 'Well sir, we think you should take ship to Aden and then ask.'

2

❦

Sweet, Just, Boyish Masters

Never since the heroic days of ancient Greece has the world had such a sweet, just, boyish master.

George Santayana (1863 – 1952)

T he linchpins of British imperial administration were the District Officers – usually young men, often callow and frequently undertrained. The responsibility thrust upon a District Officer was awesome. He was the father and mother of the people whose care he was entrusted with, and, as the historian of the Raj and former Indian Civil Servant Philip Mason says, 'the main matter for pride will be that so few among so many had so slight a need for force.' There were over 400 districts in British India, and there was a lonely District Officer in each one. Each man was imbued with a sense of duty and a built-in moral code which dictated thought processes so ingrained as to be instinctive. His job involved arbitration in land disputes, criminal investigation, court hearings, chasing unpaid taxes, and general administration. The British were justly proud that there were so few abuses of their wide-ranging and near-absolute power. There were exceptions, of course; but they were rare. The worst example is that of Brigadier-General Reginald Dyer's conduct in Amritsar in 1919, when he ordered his Gurkhas to open fire on an unarmed crowd which had gathered for a political meeting. Those were jumpy times; prior to the meeting there had been riots in the town; five Englishmen had been killed and a woman missionary assaulted. Locals had been made to crawl along the street where the assault had taken place; but now Dyer's conduct – 379 people were killed and another 1500 wounded – looked like overreaction. There were those who thought he might have averted a second Indian Mutiny. Others felt that only by the grace of God had he not precipitated one. Though he had to resign his commission, he was made an honorary member of the Brotherhood of Sikhs, and readers of *The Morning Post* got up a subscription of £25 000 for him. Paralysed by a stroke in 1938, Dyer told his daughter-in-law rather pathetically, 'I don't want to get better, I only want to die, and to know from my Maker whether I did right or wrong.'

> ∾ The question of sex between British imperial officials and their subject people was to be a matter for debate for 200 years. The relationship between master and servant changed anyway with the passing of time, and much depended upon the nature of the education and upbringing of the master.

Rule Britannia
❧

The East India College opened at Hertford in 1806 and moved to Haileybury in 1809. Here the liberal education of the future servants of the East India Company (and, later, the Indian Civil Service) was undertaken. A sister college – Haileybury's military counterpart – was founded at Addiscombe.

The Greek philosopher Plato, much admired in the eighteenth and nineteenth centuries, had envisioned the idea of a perfect state run by Guardians, men of rigorous physical and intellectual training, and brought up in the belief that they were a separate race from those they ruled. They stood apart, immune to the calls of family or wealth, ruling their charges by the light of good principles alone.

The British did not perhaps consciously follow Plato's words, but they ran very close to them. Plato taught that his Guardians should not know their parents; at Haileybury the little boys who would grow up to manage the Empire were taken from home at the age of eight and then spent three-quarters of the year away from it, taught not to mention their mothers and not allowed to use their own Christian names. It was a Spartan upbringing. It did its job; but it tended to create difficult psychological by-products as well. The stoical stiff upper lip was gained at the harmful cost of suppressing a whole range of emotions.

Recruits to the East India Company were young. Sixteen was a common age to go out, and thirteen not unknown. You could put the letters HEICS after your name – Honourable East India Company Service – and for the first four years you worked as a Writer (£10 per annum plus keep). If you made the grade you then became a Factor, doubled your income, and were in a position to start doing yourself some good. Paul Benfield, eighteen years with the Company, dismissed and reinstated three times, was nevertheless able to make £500 000.

Home leave was very rare: the voyage out could take anything from six to eighteen months in those days. Even when the voyage was short – the steamers and the Suez Canal reduced it to a mere three weeks – you were 'out' for a long time. It could be very boring at times, especially in *mofussil* (remote) postings. Bloodsports occupied the men and some of the women. Men also had the advantage of work. For the ladies, when they went out, tedium was a very real menace. Servants took care of the work, and the weather constricted other activity to a severe degree. Those who could not occupy themselves in painting, music, or translation faced purgatorial dullness.

The administrative system set up by the Company threw up some good men. Governor John Duncan not only cleaned up corruption among the British in Jessore, but also stamped out the custom of murdering unwanted daughters in his district. In 1829 Governor-General William Bentinck was instrumental in abolishing the practice of suttee (the self-immolation of a Hindu widow on her husband's funeral pyre) in Bengal, and under his auspices the murderous Thug cult was suppressed over the next few years. The Thug sect worshipped the Hindu goddess of destruction, Kali.

Governor-General Cornwallis' attempt to exclude Indians and Anglo-Indians from *all* positions of responsibility in the Company had proved impossible in practice. But real power, thought the British, still needed a solid ruling élite, racially separated from the locals. The effect this had on sexual relationships between the races was profound.

Love in a Warm Climate

❧

Before the steamship age especially, officials of the Company rarely married, and then only in middle age. Such wives as there were had a hard and dreary life – having to endure long periods of loneliness and separation. The men were devoted to their work, which they pursued with a monastic zeal. But there were exceptions, and in the early days the later Victorian prejudice regarding race and colour was not a consideration. Richard, Marquess Wellesley, and the older brother of the Duke of Wellington, was the next significant Governor-General after Cornwallis. Between 1798 and 1805 he extended British control over two-thirds of India. His first wife, by whom he had had five children before their marriage, refused to accompany him to India and he lived alone for the first two years of his administration. Thereafter he gave himself over to visiting brothels and the rest of his life included one more unhappy marriage and a string of mistresses. He died, his career abandoned and 'worn out with profligacy', in his eighty-third year.

As Resident in the volatile posting of Delhi in 1812, twenty-seven-year-old Charles Metcalfe, an enlightened old Etonian, worked for the abolition of hanging, flogging, slavery and suttee. He also had an Indian wife (or possibly mistress) for eight years, by whom he had three sons. Residents were British representatives at native Indian courts. Although they had no direct power – except where delegated to them by the princes – they had considerable influence, not only on foreign and defence policies of Indian native states, but also on internal administration as well.

A later Resident in Delhi, William Fraser, was described by the French traveller Victor Jacquemont as one who 'loved danger and fighting, but wouldn't kill anyone.' Fraser was also a great hunter, and was not averse to killing animals, dispatching eighty-four Asian lions in the course of his career. He also married six or seven Indian wives, whom he kept in a harem 'fifty leagues from Delhi', by whom he had innumerable children – 'as many as the King of Persia, but they are all Moslems or Hindus according to the religion and caste of their mammas' wrote Jacquemont. Fraser was murdered in 1835 by a young local noble who was his ward, and whom he'd had occasion strongly to reprove. There were others just as colourful. Job Charnock, who founded Calcutta between 1686 and 1690, rescued a woman from a suttee death and then married her. One of the most famous of Indian regiments, Skinner's Horse, was raised by an Anglo-Indian, James Skinner, who like Fraser ran a harem of several wives. In the early days even the East India Company itself offered a christening present of five rupees each to the children of their soldiers and their Indian wives.

When Warren Hastings was Governor-General of Bengal in the late eighteenth century, the Indian wives and mistresses of British officials appear regularly in portraits. Dr Ratnabali Chatterjee, a historian of Calcutta University, comments: 'They are by no means of the working classes. They seem to be quite rich women, and, by their gestures, their presence, their personality comes through.

And it's quite obvious that they were cherished and treated with complete respect by their husbands.'

Repressed and Aloof
ແ⁊ເ

But as the nineteenth century progressed, the sexual and racial barriers went up, and the disadvantages of the restrictive and repressive education meted out to young men began to show itself.

An extraordinary number of leaders, from Cecil Rhodes to Robert Baden-Powell either didn't marry, had unsatisfactory marriages, or had homosexual inclinations. It could perhaps even be argued that as a result of their mental training and education, some of these men had never left boyhood. Boyhood, that innocent and active phase of life untainted by the problems represented by emotional involvement with the other sex, was regarded as 'pure'. The myth of the 'happiest days of your life' grew up. A one-time Victorian Secretary of State for War, Sir John Brodrick, expressed the view at the end of his life that no responsibility he'd undertaken had ever compared with that of membership of the self-elected, prefect-like society known as 'Pop' at Eton. One of the toughest governors of the Punjab, John Lawrence, expressed his ideal of a District Officer as 'a hard active man in boots and breeches, who almost lived in the saddle, worked all day and nearly all night, ate and drank when and where he could, had no family ties, and no wife or children to hamper him.'

Of course there were exceptions: Lord Curzon, Viceroy of India from 1899 to 1905, and Sir Alfred Milner, High Commissioner of South Africa, 1897 to 1905, both had affairs (one after the other) with the very sexy romantic novelist, Elinor Glyn, of whom the anonymous verse was written:

> *Would you like to sin*
> *On a tiger skin*
> *With Elinor Glyn?*
> *Or would you prefer*
> *To err with her*
> *Upon some other kind of fur?*

Nevertheless, Milner didn't marry until 1921 when he was sixty-seven years old, having waited two decades for the married woman with whom he had fallen in love to become free; and Curzon, falling in love with his future wife in 1890, did not propose until 1892, nor marry until 1895, spending the intervening years travelling. He wrote to her in 1893, commenting on her faithfulness (she had repulsed another suitor): 'I am spared all the anxieties of what is called a great courtship, and I have merely, when the hour strikes, to enter into possession of my own.' Both men had a number of affairs, though not with local women.

In *mofussil* districts, where there was little or no other English society than, say, a handful of men comprising a district administration, it was hard for 'lesser' human beings to keep up the British aloofness which was seen as the key to successful rule without force. In the nineteenth century Captain Walters and Dr Nell lived on the best of terms until Nell went on leave, leaving Walters to look after his *bibi*, with whom the captain was also on friendly though platonic terms. Alas, the *bibi* appears to have wanted to adopt Walters and abandon Nell, who beat her. Walters seems to have interceded honourably on her behalf with Nell on his return, but the intemper-

4 Throughout the Empire local women who were employed as
nannies often became the mistresses of their male employers.
For some women this was a useful additional source of income.

5 Polo at Calcutta, 1917. In the vast majority of cases the only relationship that existed between the British and the local people was that of master and servant.

BELOW
6 Watching polo at Jaora, 1933. As the twentieth century progressed there was a degree of social integration, but this was generally restricted to upper class Indians.

ate doctor set about the captain with his fists. The ensuing brawl blew up into a scandal, and destroyed the careers of both men.

There were practical reasons, too, for discouraging too much cohabitation, especially as British rule became more formal. Burma, for example, had a more open society than India. The locals integrated well with the colonizers, and as Burma was a bit of a backwater of Empire, the rules were not so strictly enforced. Nevertheless, men who married a local girl or even cohabited with her could expect no promotion. Burmese mistresses had a reputation for intrigue, and it was difficult to remain an impartial judge or administrator if everyone else knew that your wife had your ear on behalf of her relatives. On the whole, people conformed. In 1903 out of several hundred there were only five civil servants and eight police officers with native wives.

There was one other risk attached to cohabitation: the stigma of being thought to have 'gone native'. Of course some people simply didn't give a damn about this, and many frankly preferred African or Indian society to that of their fellow countrymen. Those in the best position to indulge such feelings, however, were farmers and traders, rather than servants of Empire – though even they were held to be Britain's representatives and could risk ostracism if they persevered in their tastes. J. E. 'Chirupula' Stephenson was already married to a Ngoni girl when he became a Native Commissioner in Northern Rhodesia in 1901. He resigned in 1906 after objections had been raised to him bringing one of his Euro-African sons to visit the District Commissioner, and he settled independently in a remote valley. He was an able organizer and administrator, built 180 miles of road and opened up the area which was to become the

> ෫ Conventional Anglicanism taught devotion to duty. Sex, the unmentionable subject and the very last thing to be associated with humanity or pleasure, was driven underground. Hard work, brisk exercise, and adventurous action were the antidotes to 'impure' thoughts.

Copperbelt. He never abandoned his British culture, and fought for his country in the First World War. He acted as a safari guide for European tourists, continued to have good relations with the white administration (though not with the white women of Northern Rhodesia), married several wives, and fathered eight children.

The Aura of Empire
෫ई෫

By 1900, two million Britons lay buried in India; many of them had lived there all their lives, and learned to think of that country more as home than England. There was a great sense of responsibility to the natives of the colonized countries but little sense of usurping them in their own lands – this was rationalized by the theory that their lands would be handed back to them when they had been taught to govern them 'properly'.

But any life led in a place distant from home, with, in the early days, poor transport and communications which in turn contributed to greater isolation, in an alien culture, without much recreation, without even a regular newspaper or a bottle of cold beer now and

then, would be intolerable without some creature comforts. As ha
been mentioned, the French colonial authorities deemed it positively
beneficial to health for the isolated administrator to have
a local mistress. And the British tacitly – though unofficially –
followed suit, learning positively to enjoy the company of 'one of
the complaisant and amusing, good-tempered and good-mannered
daughters of the East', or 'sleeping dictionary', as she was often
referred to – there being no better way to learn a language than to
have an affair with someone whose native tongue it is.

If your tastes were other than conventional, the colonies would
provide without demure. As one officer put it early this century: 'I
naturally prefer to satisfy myself with a woman, a friend and a lady
of my own class; but in the absence of the best I gladly take the next
best available, down the scale from a lady for whom I do not care, to
prostitutes of all classes and colours, men, boys and animals, melons
and masturbation.' In Sarawak, the 'white rajahs' of the Brooke
family encouraged intermarriage, more or less, and certainly
cohabitation with local girls, well into the twentieth century. In
Africa, where District Officers were, if anything, even more isolated
from society and from each other than in the Raj, concubinage was
quite usual. So common did it become, in fact, that in the end officialdom had to take notice of it and act. And the British view, in
contrast to the French, held such practice to be 'injurious and
dangerous'.

The trigger was a scuffle in 1905 between a British official in
Kenya called Hubert Silberrad, and the native policeman husband of
one of his black mistresses. It might never have been noticed had it
not been for the officious interference of a neighbour, a certain

W. S. Routledge, who found Silberrad's general conduct so immoral (it was probably no more so than that of a hundred other British officials) that he took the matter to the Governor. From there it escalated out of all proportion, occasioning parliamentary debate and letters to *The Times*, and incidentally bringing poor Silberrad's career to a grinding halt. Its outcome was a Circular, reluctantly issued by the Secretary of State for the Colonies, Lord Crewe, containing guidelines for sexual conduct (or rather, the avoidance of it) for all colonial officials. The Crewe Circular was in force from 1909 to 1934, and was damaging in that it could be evoked to terminate the careers of otherwise excellent administrators who had done nothing more than give way to their natural sexual appetites. In one sense, it was symptomatic of the popular and increasingly restrictive thinking *vis-à-vis* sex in the late Victorian age, which spilled over into Edwardian times and later, and which was, ultimately, damaging. The good news was that in the field, those whom experience had taught the value of a more liberal attitude, were able to interpret the letter of the Circular with a certain generosity.

The aim remained to turn out men who could hold up the aura of the Empire as District Officers. But the imperial ideal was hard to keep up. Douglas Stanton-Ife worked out of the small Indian town of Aurangabad in the province of Bihar: 'I remember that one of my superiors was asked what he'd got up to in Sitamuri, which was his first subdivision. "Oh," he said, "grand place, Sitamuri, I worked all day and fucked all night."' 'Well,' adds Stanton-Ife a little sadly, 'that was not my experience.'

Stanton-Ife recalls: 'The Raj had its reputation for authority and most people accepted that. And for a time at least, I was the embodiment of that authority in my own particular area, Malaka. I had no private life. Everything I did was known. I was very lonely and there were many frustrations. I had one good Indian friend but no female company whatsoever.'

In such circumstances, temptation could strike in odd places. For Stanton-Ife it was in his local courtroom:

> I think it was Section 353 – criminal assault on a woman with intent to outrage her modesty. The doctor present had to be a woman, and she gave evidence regarding the attack on the plaintiff. Well, the doctor was very neat and looked very nice, and spoke very well. And I think I would normally have asked her to come and have tea with me, and I think she would probably have accepted. But because of the fact that the Raj was so personal, because one had no private life, I didn't dare do so, because I thought it would be bound to get round the bazaar, and if it didn't endanger my reputation, it would certainly harm hers.

The Army was in the same position. Colonel Wallace Pryke was a subaltern in a British regiment in India during the 1930s:

> If you're going to be an occupying army it is really probably best for you to remain away from any local influences. You were trained to support the civil power and you might have been called upon to open fire on civilians in times of unrest; so that you really had to remain apart if you were going to be completely objective about what you were going to do. Of course during formal entertainments and things like that you would meet Indian people sometimes – those in authority, those with local influence; but you didn't mix with them socially very much.

As for sentimental attachments, Pryke could recall stories of officers who had married Indian women and then been transferred. Sometimes they would be transferred out of harm's way before getting too involved. The commanding officer's permission was required in order to wed, and that would give him enough warning to intervene.

But attachments weren't altogether to be avoided. Pryke remembers that:

> Kashmir was quite a Mecca for young officers to go to. You normally hired a houseboat and were looked after by a Kashmiri family. You could go boating on the lake in little canoes with heart-shaped paddles. It was all very romantic up there and most delightful. I remember that on one of the lakes a nice party was got together by a senior officer, and I found myself paired off with a very delightful blonde, and we had a lovely time together. Sadly it came to an end because I discovered from photographs she showed me that her family was completely Indian. I had very mixed feelings at the time because if you're fond of somebody and find yourself in a situation like that it's rather difficult. I also had to remember that I was in the army as a professional soldier. I'd joined up very much indeed with the object of making a professional career out of it, and faced with the prospect of anything interfering with that made one think very seriously. I'd had a very strong sense of duty knocked into me by my family, and in the army as a young officer, and I'm afraid that in the end, duty came first.

The spectre of racial difference hovered over Wallace Pryke as it had done over Martin Sharp. But the gulf was fundamentally social and political, not sexual. The important thing was not to get involved with a woman who might expect a permanent relationship. Historian Ratnabali Chatterjee observes that the white men would 'confine themselves to women whom they could mate with and then leave. These would generally be working-class women. In the case of the tea planters, it would be the labouring women on the plantation. In the jute mills, they would be factory workers. Otherwise, it would be women servants.

> 🐦 'As far as the British were concerned, I think that it was part of their code of ethics from the eighteenth century onwards to regard all working-class women as sexually available – at home as well as abroad.'

For the ruling British élite, such women were faceless, they were there to do a service.'

Major-General Uday Dubey was one of seven sons of a prosperous Kashmiri family, all of whom joined the British Indian army as officers. The young Uday was one of the first to be sent to Sandhurst for training. As such he became theoretically a British officer, entitled to the overseas allowances enjoyed by his British comrades and sharing the same quarters. It was a difficult transformation, nonetheless negotiated successfully by many young Indians. It was also an opportunity to observe the traditional methods of maintaining face and satisfying libido at the same time. Uday remembers:

71

In the Indian army, the British officers had bearers. Everybody had a bearer and in quite a number of cases, especially people who had been here a long time, or were bachelors, they always got women. Even grass-cutter women: they often had very good physiques, beautiful busts, beautiful everything. They would be half-naked, cutting the grass and the British officer would look and recognize a nice thing, and tell the bearer, 'How much money?', and the bearer would fetch the girl.

The bearers studied their Sahib, they knew absolutely what Sahib wants, what his tastes were.

These things were known, and you saw people coming and you saw people going. And you saw jingling-wingling going on in the room – these people wore all sorts of noisy things, bangles on their arms and legs. And when they're moving about naturally there's a lot of noise. You would be living in the next room and you would sometimes cough and say, 'All well?' And they would say, 'No, no, don't bother.' And so you knew always, but they wouldn't tell you. And you wouldn't want to ask. These are their own personal matters.

Anglo-African Relationships

⊰§⊱

In India these things took effect over generations. In Africa, it happened more quickly. By 1900, the British had taken over a huge new addition to its Empire, comprising the greater part of central and southern Africa, and all the same questions re-emerged. As a girl in the 1920s, Henrietta Fanshawe lived on the Gold Coast, where her father was a Provincial Commissioner:

> I hadn't the slightest doubt that my father was in Africa to do
> good to the African. It was inherent in the atmosphere: that is

what those young men went out there for; nothing else. They led miserable lives. I was struck by the fact that everything was late. Their letters arrived late; their newspapers were late. They weren't allowed to have African mistresses, even. My father saw to it that they lived two to a hut to keep each other company at least; but they led austere lives to the nth degree.

Many of the young men were the sons of clergymen – a policy encouraged in Colonial Service recruitment in the dubious belief that this would promote sexual 'purity'. Whether it worked, records do not reveal. But the Crewe Circular had to be seen to be having some effect.

Terence Gavaghan attended a Jesuit school in the 1930s and was attracted to the African Colonial Service from an early age, though he came from an Indian Civil Service family background and was born in India. In his early twenties he was posted to Kenya:

My very first experience was to go to a district about 17 000 square miles in size, with a population of perhaps 270 000. I had a very up-market boss, highly intelligent, with a wife who was equally so – a perfect pairing of intelligence and goodwill. Unfortunately he became diabetic and had to leave. Then the Number Two, whose nickname was Double Diamond Sculls, contracted cerebral malaria. He too disappeared and I found myself without language, without resources, without training, except for a little bit in the Ulster Rifles, in command of this whole apparatus – magistracy, accountancy, agriculture, road-building, locust control – everything. I remember that I learnt a speech in Swahili by heart and it caused everybody present to fall about, just to hear perfect Swahili emanating from such an ignorant person . . . .

Once again, companionship was a problem, though he met with little sympathy from the Governor, who simply told him, 'Balls, Gavaghan, I've never heard such unutterable balls in all my life. You're surrounded by tens of thousands of people – how can you be lonely?'

The Crewe Circular had fallen by the wayside by the time Terence Gavaghan took up his post, though its effects were still felt, and racial distinctions were still firmly in place. In official minutes, for example, European recipients were addressed as 'Esquire' and Africans as 'Mister'. Such distinctions were not even blinked at: they had become conventions. But the distinctions were no barrier to sex, as Gavaghan explains:

> I remember one particular girl with great pleasure – she was half Arab and half Nandi. We enjoyed a happy association which lasted a number of years; but she lived in her own village with her family and I lived in my house alone. That was the protocol of the times, if you like. It was an unspoken thing that she wouldn't call on me openly, and wouldn't come to the house if I had a dinner party in progress, for example .... I do recall that once she came to my house near the lake and we passed a pleasant time before dinner. Then I said, 'Look, I'm terribly sorry, but I've got to go out to dinner.' I think it was with the chief medical officer and his wife and a group of other people. I remember at the time wondering at dinner with an internal smile what my fellow guests would say if they knew whom I'd just left and whom I was looking forward to going back to.
>
> I didn't find African women more or less attractive than others. There is no knowing what makes people attracted to one another, and I never looked at an African woman with the

idea that she was much sexier, or more passionate, or more responsive, or more beautiful than any other woman whom I found attractive or who might have found me attractive. The attraction was to the person, regardless of race.

These relationships were sentimental attachments, not business contracts. As a young man, Gavaghan was moved around a lot and had other affairs, but never does he give the impression that they were casual or without personal meaning. None was over quickly, either.

> I remember there was one young woman who was tall, very dark, dressed in long, very concealing clothing, with a silk shawl over her head. She used to come round selling baskets. I was very struck by her, and it appeared to be reciprocated. We didn't exchange money and she used to come and visit me in my house overlooking the valley as often as it could be arranged. Sometimes I would buy her stuff, and she would bring me eggs for my kitchen, which was quite a normal, mutually respecting thing to do. I remember practising my romantic Swahili on her. I would use expressions which frankly I had to study out of a book to express to her the sort of almost childish emotions which I could conjure up by translation into this foreign language which I wasn't used to using in an amatory sense at all. I think it amused her. And she was great fun to be with. I remember her laughter, her conversation, gossip, chat, intimacy. Her gossamer hair, her delicate physique. I remember one overlapping front tooth, as if it were yesterday.

But she had her life and Gavaghan had his. They did not live together, nor did he visit her at her home. Such a thing might have interfered with her social standing and marital expectations.

Gavaghan was more than usually sensitive to the delicate balance of Anglo-African relationships, but he remained in his own camp. Rising to the rank of District Commissioner, he saw to it that his subordinates recognized the boundaries, too.

Such relationships as he and many others enjoyed were perhaps not designed to last forever, and parting affected both sides. After the death of her husband, Margaret Wiarimu worked as a prostitute in Nairobi. The white men would give her food. There, during the Second World War, she met and fell in love with a European. 'I was so close to him. If he had given me a child I would have kept it because we loved each other so much. He never came to my house, but I could go and live with him sometimes for up to a week. I was so fond of him. He was kind to me, and gave me sugar and things like that for my mother, and cigarettes for my brothers. But he was jealous of me; he didn't want to see me go with other men.' In the end he returned to England. 'It was very painful when he left. We had known each other for years. I went to collect my things from his house when he had gone and I felt so sad when I packed them. But then I continued moving with the other men.'

It was not necessary to conceal one's relationships, though one didn't advertise them either. Terence Gavaghan says,

> The relationships happened. I did not carelessly expose them to view but I did not keep them quiet. Nobody ever asked me about them within my own circle – after all, I knew about what my colleagues were doing, too. To a certain extent, we had that in common. Not that I measured the performance of my colleagues, as it were. I would know which ones were likely to be having affairs, and which were self-deniers. You could also

hazard a guess about which ones were – what's the polite word? – onanists, and which were heading towards a homo-sexual relationship, too.

Crossing the Dividing Line

&

At root for the British there always remained the preservation of power and the reputation of officials – plus of course the usual concerns about corruption. Douglas Stanton-Ife recalls another time in India when he was obliged to resist temptation:

> There was a widow who came forward when I was a bit older and stationed at Palamu. I think she actually wrote me a letter in which she told me that her daughter was unmarried, and that as I was unmarried as well this seemed a pity from every-one's point of view. And so she thought that I ought to meet her daughter socially. Actually I think the cultural differences would have been so insuperable as to make marriage impos-sible, but there was another aspect: the widow was engaged in litigation. Not in my court – that was the criminal court – but in the civil court. Even so, I don't think it would have been wise for me to start carrying on with the daughter of a litigant.

The higher the official, the greater the risk of his being found out and dismissed – less on account of disgrace than because he might have misappropriated government funds or equipment for the benefit of his native mistress or her family. So maybe Douglas Stanton-Ife was right: it was better to be safe than sorry; though he does admit rather wistfully that 'I think I could have had, perhaps without doing too much harm to the Raj, rather more fun than I did. But this was one of the sacrifices that I thought I was making for the

Raj. I knew before I went that I would have to work for many years in virtual solitude, and that there would be frustrations and emotional difficulties. It was important not to make oneself vulnerable; but looking back, I do rather regret that I didn't think it was possible to have more to do with Indian ladies than I did.'

To make contact with the local women apart from the servants, Raj colonists had to cross the dividing line between their cantonment and the Indian town. There was, as we have seen, little contact between the foreigners and high-caste Indian women, and the proprieties were observed to a ludicrous degree. Historian Dr Chatterjee describes how it was in the nineteenth century: 'Quite a lot of middle-class Bengalis came to Calcutta to live, and they built themselves houses which were very colonial in their architecture, but in order to adapt them to their own needs they had inner and outer courtyards built – the women remained in the former. And if the women should go bathing in the Ganges, for example, they'd get into a bathing machine and the whole thing would be dipped into the river!'

Even so, some of the *bibis* came from the upper echelons of Indian society – according to Dr Chatterjee 'women who were from impoverished upper-class families, or who'd been thrown over by an earlier patron, or by a nawab who could no longer afford to keep her.' But most of the casual acquaintances were struck with women street workers; not necessarily professional prostitutes; but milk-vendors, grass-cutters, cotton-weavers, sweepers. And such women had sold their favours traditionally, it wasn't something that just happened with the advent of the British.

The British may have ridden roughshod over the subtler traditional Indian nuances between different types of prostitute – no

Indian would have failed to distinguish between a nautch dancer, a *devadasi*, and a streetwalker, for example. But their arrival brought some interesting changes, as Dr Chatterjee points out: 'The British intervention in India is to be regarded in terms of its cultural effects to have been a modernizing factor. It not only opened the gates of English education to the Indian male, but to Indian women as well. From that you begin to see the emergence of the middle-class woman, who later entered the professions. One unfortunate side-effect, however, was that Indian men grew afraid that their women might get out of hand and so there was a conservative reaction . . . . I think the British also confirmed and colluded in this Indian male fear.'

Emancipated white women who came to work in India as missionaries or social reformers muddied the waters further by providing role models for their Indian sisters.

Pig-sticking and Cold Showers
ॐ

If Indian society was hidebound by convention, it was matched by that of the colonists, especially within the ranks of the Army. Colonel Wallace Pryke recalls that: 'The atmosphere in the mess was I suppose a bit more formal than you'd get in England. You didn't really speak to senior officers unless they spoke to you first. And of course you dressed every night except for Saturday and Sunday in full mess kit for formal dinner.' Soldiers married late, often because marriage allowances didn't become available until an officer was about thirty; but marriage in general was discouraged. There weren't the facilities to house a lot of wives and there was a general feeling that a bachelor made a better fighting man.

Sport was regarded as the great sublimator. Wallace Pryke remembers:

> Pig-sticking, for example – it's pretty dangerous to go after a wild boar with a lance on a horse across the countryside in typical boar country, where the grass was probably up to your waist – you couldn't see where you were going, so you had to have a very good horse. Pig-sticking was a favourite of the cavalry and gunner regiments, but we had a pack of hounds of a kind – bit of a mixed bunch – and went after jackal. It was quite a horsy world and as one mixed with the cavalry a lot one was put through a cavalry course as soon as one arrived.
>
> It was a very masculine atmosphere. You could get leave pretty easily to go hunting but it was a different story if you wanted to go off to Delhi, say. I think that was reasonable. The games and sports developed you and gave you a sense of the country, seeing the local population when you were out shooting; whereas going to Delhi and sampling the fleshpots there didn't necessarily make you a better officer. I wouldn't say that we were ever encouraged not to go out, but it became a sort of unwritten convention among the young officers – this was in the thirties don't forget – that you didn't mix socially, particularly with Indian ladies. They were not invited to your mess nor were they normally allowed into your club either. This may sound rather drastic under modern circumstances, but the British were there very much with an aim in view, and that was keeping the peace for the whole of India, and remaining apart from the local community helped us to do our job.

But perhaps sport wasn't as effective as all that in keeping young officers' minds on their duty, as Wallace Pryke observes, 'There's

ABOVE
7 Colonel Wallace Pryke on a
hunting expedition in an isolated
part of the North-West Frontier,
India. Sporting activities such as
hunting were regarded as an
excellent means of sublimating
pent-up sexual frustrations.

RIGHT
8 Douglas Stanton-Ife, who found
working as a District Officer in a
small Indian town 'very lonely'
with 'many frustrations'.

THE SPHERE

AN ILLUSTRATED NEWSPAPER FOR THE HOME.

Volume XII. No. 157.   London, January 24, 1903.   Price Sixpence.

ABOVE

9 Lord Curzon, sketched for *The Sphere* in 1903. Curzon was a firm and unyielding believer in keeping the natives in their place, though this gave him many a diplomatic headache.

RIGHT

10 Memsahib in action: Lady Curzon on a visit to Hydrabad in 1902.

11 During his often lonely postings for the African
Colonial Administration, Terence Gavaghan had
several happy relationships with local women. In his
own words, 'The attraction was to the person,
regardless of race.'

no doubt this fitness had a slight drawback in that it made people so fit that it possibly made them wish to have female company in an even stronger way than they might have done if they hadn't been so fit. This was always a problem with us and the lack of female company was a very difficult thing to handle in India. We had to be fit to do our work, and it did keep morale up, what with inter-regimental games and so forth. But the only advice the doctors could give us with regard to the other business was to take as cold a bath as you could get in the Indian climate and then take even more exercise.'

But it wasn't always possible to rein in one's feelings completely. Len Brooks joined the Army as a school-leaver in the 1930s to avoid the dole. He remembers a discipline 'second only to the Foreign Legion' – eight hours a day of training with Thursday afternoons off for fatigue duties. But there was some time for socializing.

He was posted to Hong Kong, and there he was introduced to the practice of taxi-dancing:

> You bought a dollar's worth of tickets at ten cents a ticket, and all the girls were lined up in the dance hall – it was always above a shop – and there might be a Filipino band. And you'd pick a girl you liked and ask her to dance and give her a ticket. Or the whole roll, if you wanted to dance with her a lot. They were just normal girls and that's how they'd earn their money; they weren't all prostitutes. But you might make a date with one, take her to the pictures. They were lovely girls. The weather was so hot and humid, but they were cool; it felt like you had an ice-cream alongside of you – you was cooled down.

There was one particular girl who worked in a tourist shop with whom Len fell in love, and she with him. 'She looked like a doll, seemed so fragile. Everything about her was attractive. She was half Indian and half Chinese. About five foot two. I used to buy stuff in her shop and finally I plucked up enough courage to ask her to the pictures, and to my surprise she said she would.' He went out with her for as long as he was in Hong Kong. None of his mates ever censured him – they were going out with Chinese girls too – and nor did the officers. 'They never said nothing. At that time a soldier wasn't allowed to get married until he was twenty-one. Some people did get married out there, but they also found work and settled down instead of coming home.'

The end came when his regiment was ordered to Shanghai at short notice. He borrowed a bicycle to go and say goodbye, sure that he'd be able to return to her soon. He gave her all the pay he'd just received. 'I felt completely lost, leaving her. I thought I'd lost something. I wrote and she wrote, but our letters kept crossing and a lot of what we said was censored – whether by the British or the Japanese, I don't know . . . . I would have married her if I'd got the chance. I intended to if I'd got back to Hong Kong. I could've joined the police or got on the prison staff or something.'

The course of the war never took him back to Hong Kong. He was posted from Shanghai to the Sudan, and then to France. Captured by the Germans, he escaped and spent the rest of the war fighting with the Polish Resistance. Back home, he married and settled down. He has not heard any more of the Chinese girl in the sixty years since he last saw her.

Team Spirit and Dancing Girls
❧

Team spirit could sometimes keep the demons of the flesh at bay. Rupert Mayne, whose family involvement in India goes back to the eighteenth century, says, '*esprit de corps*, discipline, friendship, example, leadership, patriotism – these were the things we learned at Wellington [the public school which traditionally prepares pupils for Sandhurst Military Academy].' He went to India in the 1930s to work in a jute mill. There was a good deal of socializing in Calcutta, but little mixing, except, notably, at the 300 Club. It was run by a man called Boris who'd been sauce chef to the old Tsar, and who'd fled east after the Russian Revolution. As Mayne explains 'The 300 Club was open to all comers. There was no colour bar, and during the war it was absolutely the place to go.' It provided the opportunity to meet Indian women informally too, of course, but one didn't get involved: 'There were some marriages, but then you had the strain of not being able to join a club. If you were a member of the Saturday Club, for example, you had to resign when you got married, and be re-elected again with your wife.'

Brigadier Tom Collins also remembers team spirit as the concept most dinned into him at the prep. school he attended before Haileybury. As for girls – 'We weren't interested in them. We were interested in playing cricket and football and doing regimental things. And it wasn't quite the form to be popping off with girls.' That was in Jamaica, where there was a sizable white community. Later, in Shanghai, where there was also a large number of Europeans, Collins did start to dance with women in the nightclubs. 'We danced with the Europeans because we thought that was the right thing to do; anyhow, they could dance the same way as we did. But we used to find that it was rather easier to dance with Chinese ladies because they were only about three feet high and if you got in a muddle you picked them up and got out of the muddle and put them down again and got on with it.'

Tom Collins' grandfather, an army doctor, had a more gratifying experience involving dancing girls in Morocco in 1890. 'The sultan's chief wife was ill. I can't tell you exactly what my grandfather did, I expect he gave her some Army Number 9 pills or something like that. Anyhow, in a couple of days she was her dancing self again. And the Sultan of Morocco was so pleased that he gave my grandfather a horse and two dancing girls. Alas, the hand of British protocol decreed that he could keep the horse but must return the girls.'

As we have seen, once in India, protocol's hand indeed fell heavily on the Army officer. As Tom Collins says: 'In India what we had to do was behave, because they looked up to us, we were sahibs, and it was very important to behave properly the whole time. That was absolutely essential.'

But keeping oneself apart wasn't always sensible. Lieutenant-Colonel Gautam Sharma of the Indian Army remembers that during the Second World War, Hindu Indian soldiers were issued with bully beef – this nearly a century after the Indian Mutiny had been sparked by a similar insult to their religion – though at that time the cartridges greased with animal fat had been withdrawn: 'We had to live as they lived, and behave as they wanted us to behave. They never wanted to learn anything from us. We had to learn all their customs, and there was this thing: anyone who spoke out against the British was a marked man, and dismissed. Even their histories of the Mutiny tell that all Indians were traitors, from Bahadur Shah Zafar downward.'

On the other hand, Dr John Sarkies, an Army Medical Officer stationed in India in the late 1930s, can remember a more relaxed atmosphere: 'Secunderabad was a very mixed station and we all mixed together – the officers shared the clubs, and the NCOs shared the canteens. I do remember doing a very tactless thing once – my wife and I turned up to a fancy-dress ball as nigger minstrels. I shudder to think of it now – we called ourselves Down and South. But no Indian took offence. They laughed. I suppose they thought I was just a callow young officer fresh from England – just off the ice, as they used to say – and they were quite right.'

White Man's Dignity

❧

Despite all precautions, the white man's dignity could some-times slip. Roly Armour went out to Kenya as a young man in the early 1930s to work for the telegraph company. An uncle of his, Captain W. A. C. Hughes, was already farming there, and this iras-cible man was unconventional enough to be living quite openly with a Kikuyu woman, earning himself the nickname 'Black' Hughes. The meeting place for the local settler community was Barry's Hotel at Thompson's Falls. As Armour recounts:

> I do remember one episode there. He picked a row with a neighbour in the bar, and it got so hot that they came to blows and they went outside to the yard to sort it out between them. Barry rang the police and the European policemen came with a couple of black *askaris* to break it up. I remember one of the

policemen coming back into the bar afterwards holding up a funny looking thing. He didn't know what it was, but it was hairy. And he said to Barry, 'What sort of animal is this?' And of course it was my uncle's toupee. It had come off in the scuffle. It was a new one I'd brought out for him from England. He was as bald as a coot apart from that.'

Lack of knowledge of the language could spare your dignity. It was common for the white colonist on his or her travels to be carried by locals in a kind of hammock called a *mshela* – Mary Hall, the great Victorian explorer, used one. So did Kit Mullans's father – but he weighed seventeen stone: 'There'd be about half-a-dozen to carry my father, I can tell you, and they used to groan when he got on board. And if you knew the language, which very few people in Africa seemed to master, you knew the song they sang as they walked was all about this great fat man they had to carry up the mountain.'

British settlers were not averse to laying down the law in no uncertain manner in Africa, and sometimes ruled their vast estates like petty kingdoms. One such larger-than-life example of this was Ewart Grogan, a soldier-adventurer who by 1912 ended up with well over 180 000 acres of white highland farmland in Kenya – more even than the patriarch of Kenya settlers, Lord Delamere. In the course of Grogan's long life his voice was consistently raised in support of settler interests, but his attitudes are instructive. His youngest daughter, Jane Elliot – whom he cordially disliked – says, 'I don't think he really seriously envisaged that the African had any role to play at all. He was fond of Africans and was a good employer, but I don't think he thought that they had any aspirations, and a lot of people shared his view. The Mau Mau uprising (1952–57) came as a complete shock because most people had no idea at all of what had been seething beneath the surface.' (The Mau Mau was the secret society of the Kikuyu.) In fact Grogan might have been forewarned, as he had struck up a friendship with the young Kenyan nationalist leader, Tom Mboya; though his recipe for dealing with the Mau Mau in 1952 – not taken up – was ferocious: he proposed that 100 captives should be taken into the northern desert, and that there twenty-five of them should be hanged, while the rest were to be given starvation rations and left to walk back to the Kikuyu with the news.

It is hard to understand how the British – or any other colonizer – can have imagined that he would not cause resentment in the end. Even the means of introducing European civilization, the concept of money, for example, were often crude. In Kenya, a hut tax was introduced to show the locals what money was. You paid a British official a tax in order to be allowed to live in your own home. Kenyan farmer Kibe Muciiri was on the receiving end of this: 'We did not have money in those days, and if a man did not have money, he had to give the white man his goat. The white man paid him two shillings for his goat, and then took back the two shillings because that was the tax. If you couldn't pay, they just burned your hut down.'

But the colonizers believed they were in the right, and Doing Good, and that was really the end of it.

3

❧❦

Black Peril

I hope you have not had visions of me
plundered and massacred by the crazy
darweesh who has caused the destruction of
Gau and three other villages. I assure you we
are quite quiet here and moreover have
arranged matters for our defence if Achmet el
Tayib should honour us with a visit. The heat
has just set in, thermometer 89° today, of
course I am much better, fatter and cough less.

Letter to Mrs Ross, 1865
Lucie Duff-Gordon (1821 – 1869)

In 1911 the King Emperor George V came to Delhi to celebrate
his coronation. Delhi would replace Calcutta as the capital of
British India the following year, and in the twilight of Empire
the young architect Edwin Lutyens was about to start work on his
magisterial building of a new city there.

The Durbar was immense, and like much of the British pomp in
the Empire, the aim was to stress the power and permanence of the
Raj. With only 1000 administrators and just 60 000 British soldiers
to govern a population of 200 million the gathering was perhaps a
necessary confidence trick, because from the start British control
was never unquestioned. There were frequent riots and political

arguments. Even when the situation seemed calm, there was an underlying unease.

As always, the status quo had to be maintained and appearances kept up. Life continued in its rigid routine despite the depredations of the Indian climate: 'In cold weather, Calcutta was almost pleasant,' writes the historian Michael Edwardes, 'though some of the older men found it positively frigid and insisted on great fires. Most of the houses, unfortunately, did not have fireplaces. When the hot weather came round, the viceregal caravan moved off to the rarefied heights of Simla. Families who were due for leave departed for home on the steamers of the P & O, whose departures and passenger lists were chronicled in the newspapers. Everyone who could do so left for the hills.'

Calcutta in the hot weather, for those who had to stay there, was quite something. Grass screens went up in the shops and Indians were employed to keep them moist. Cholera put in its seasonal appearance, and the brain-fever bird kept up its maddening chatter all day.

A couple might start their day with a dawn ride, and then the husband would leave for the office, but by noon the heat made it impossible for anyone to work. Until two it was impossible to do anything but take a siesta, followed by lunch, then perhaps a little more work, after which followed 'a bathe and a breath of torrid air before dinner at eight and bed at half-past ten.'

Shrinking Violets?

ৰ্ছ৯ৈ৯

Even by Victorian times there were a large number of capable and independent European women working actively in India and Africa as doctors, nurses, missionaries and social reformers.

Some were busybodies, others were self-righteous, but all were able to look after themselves. The theosophist Annie Besant championed the cause of Indian nationalism in her later years; Annette Akroyd Beveridge opposed the wholesale imposition of Western culture; Margaret Cousins was an active proponent of birth-control; Caroline Chisholm encouraged the emigration of women and children to Australia to stabilize society there; and the formidable Angela Burdett-Coutts, daughter of the banker, used much of her vast fortune to promote culture and industry in Australia and Africa.

At the other end of the scale, when the erotic dancer Maud Allan threatened to take her act to India in 1910, there was an outcry: that would have done more than undermine the image the British wished to present to the Indians of their women, and the worst of it was that young Indians would be allowed to buy tickets. Petitions poured into the Viceroy's office complaining.

> ❧ Gertrude Bell, an accomplished Arabist, virtually ran the Arab Bureau in the early years of the twentieth century, and as Oriental Secretary for Iraq controlled the destiny of that country:
>
> *From Trebizon to Tripolis*
> *She rolls the Pashas flat,*
> *And tells them what to think of this,*
> *And what to think of that.*

Women of more modest achievements were given their due – by the men, but their role was well-defined, and it was convenient to keep them within it: 'It is the Englishwoman,' wrote the German traveller and diplomat Baron von Hübner admiringly at the end of the nineteenth century, 'courageous, devoted, well-educated, well-trained – the Christian, the guardian angel of the domestic hearth – who by her magic wand has brought about this wholesome trans-formation.' He was talking about British society in India. The presence of white ladies had made it far more polite. From the 1860s it had become increasingly *infra dig.* to cohabit with a native girl.

> ৯ Memsahibs going out in the nineteenth century were advised to wear the London fashions of two years ago, in order not to upset the reigning resident establishment by showing them up. On the other hand the export home of Eastern scholarship and even fashion had begun in the more relaxed eighteenth century. Although Indian dress and food were not considered *de rigueur* in the Raj, the memsahibs were responsible for their export to England, where they were fashionable at least in London – curried fish being regarded as a healthy food. The ruling English élite may have rejected Indian food, dress, material and artefacts, presumably out of fear of being thought to have 'gone native', but in 1875 Arthur Lasenby Liberty began importing Indian jewellry with great success

There were other facets to explain this change in society. The Indian Mutiny of 1857 caused a gulf to open between the British and the Indians which had not existed before. Added to that, the regular, reliable and fast sailings from England which started after the opening of the Suez Canal meant that lots of young ladies could come over to India. Some came to join husbands; some came to find husbands. The cool season was the time of the visitation of the so-called 'fishing fleet'.

The stereotypical memsahib was indolent, intriguing, uninterested in India, despotic to her servants, snobbish, racist, and bored. Some will certainly have been like this. Others must have endured quiet and heroic struggles against those very things. Women were to a certain extent trapped in the role their men had created for them: the 'pure' sister, mother, or wife, guardian of her children, symbol of innocence, the delicate flower that needed the strong arms of a man to protect her – these were Victorian preoccupations which bordered on obsession.

Even the stereotype of the memsahib was a male invention, and though there are sympathetic and even poignant descriptions of English roses who have transmuted into memsahibs, it has to be added that such descriptions rather beg the question whether sahibs themselves were not prone to a similar mental putrefaction:

> graduated, qualified, sophisticated . . . she has lost her pretty colour – that always goes first, and has gained a shadowy ring under each eye – that always comes afterwards . . . her world is the personal world of Anglo-India, and outside of it I believe she does not think at all. She is growing dull to India too, which is about as sad a thing as any. She sees no more the supple savagery of the Pathan in the market-place, the bowed

reverence of the Mussulman praying in the sunset, the early
morning mists lifting among the domes and palms of the city.
She had acquired for the Aryan inhabitant a certain strong irri-
tation, and she believes him to be nasty in all his ways . . . . She
is a memsahib like any other!

Few men would have found Kipling's tough and self-sufficient Mrs
Hauksbee sympathetic, and even in her fictional world she leads a
lonely and rather barren life. Despite the thousand examples to the
contrary, men still liked to think of their women as shrinking violets, there to be protected. This protectivenesss took various forms.
In 1926 a British bishop argued that 'the majority of films which are
chiefly from America are of sensational and daring murders, crimes
and divorces, and, on the whole, degrade the white woman in the
eyes of the Indians.' This was not the beginning of the debate; two
years earlier, *The Times* had published an article explaining the danger of showing such films to Indian audiences:

> The native never seems to grow up mentally, and the average
> audience at these picture theatres is, therefore, composed of
> those who are mature in body and very immature indeed in
> mind. To them are exhibited 'sex films' made in American stu-
> dios, and films in which violence is the main theme. With these
> may be sandwiched a comic film showing a white man carrying
> out a series of ridiculous antics. The result is inevitable, and a
> little while ago there was definite proof that the abduction by
> natives of an officer's wife was suggested by a serial film in
> which scenes of violence occurred.

The Times was taking up a cudgel which had already been wielded by *The
Westminster Gazette* in 1921, which ran an article of rather more subtlety:

A visitor to an average cinema show in England will be treated to a more or less sensational drama in which somebody's morals have gone decidedly wrong, a thrilling but impossible cowboy film and, of course, will be afforded an opportunity to appreciate (or not) our marvellous sense of humour as displayed by Charlie Chaplin squirting inoffending people with soda syphons, or breaking innumerable windows.

Now imagine the effect of such films on the Oriental mind. Like us, the Indian goes to see the 'movies', but is not only impressed by the story of the film, but by the difference in dress, in customs, and in morals. He sees our women on the films in scanty garb. He marvels at our heavy, infantile humour – his own is on a higher and more intellectual level. He forms his own opinions of our morals during the nightly unrolled dramas of unfaithful wives and immoral husbands, our lightly broken promises, our dishonoured laws. It is difficult for the Britisher in India to keep up his dignity, and to extol or to enforce moral laws which the native sees lightly disregarded by the Britons themselves in the 'picture palaces'.

This of course was a considerably greater threat than little Indian boys reading *The Arabian Nights*, and censorship was liberally applied – not just to 'indecent' scenes, but to lines which might be of political import, for example, 'We are fighting for freedom from tyranny as your country once did', cut from the film *Hutch of the USA* in 1926. But the strain of protecting the British name in India, and British women (who were sometimes quite unwilling to be protected), had been felt for a long time before that by administrators.

Powerful Attractions
◆§§◆

In 1893, the Maharajah of Patiala married one Miss Florry Bryan. Before he did so, Patiala had asked through an intermediary what the reaction of the Viceroy might be to such a union. Lord Lansdowne was direct: 'Europeans will certainly object to treat this lady as a suitable consort for a ruler in your position. They will also resent the idea of a European lady being married to a Native Chief as one of a number of wives.' The issue here was twofold. It was a mixed marriage, and that was bad; but to compound matters, Florry Bryan was very far from being 'out of the right drawer' socially for an aristocrat, even though she belonged to the ruling race. Lansdowne's dictum didn't put Patiala off, nor did it discourage similar mixed marriages. Lord Curzon a few years later was horrified to learn that the young Rajah of Jind had married 'the daughter of a professional aeronaut of low character and of Dutch or German origin.' It was never established what Olive Monalescu's roots really were. The surname is Romanian; the *Simla News* gave it out that she was the daughter of a Bombay barber and a female parachutist.

As if that wasn't enough for the harassed Curzon, the Rajah of Pudukkottai now applied for permission to attend Queen Victoria's 1897 Jubilee celebrations in London. Permission was refused, because he was a young, extravagant man, and the Powers That Were feared his marrying a European woman.

Behind all this lay the constant need to safeguard the social distance between the ruling British and the rest of India. Much to Curzon's chagrin, his efforts in this direction were constantly undermined by the friendly reception given to those Indians who did visit England and mainland Europe. The Rajah of Karpurthala was only a 'third-class' ruler, and privately Curzon suspected his morals, but he was not only received by the President of the French Republic, but also had a special reception and lunch at Buckingham Palace. At the Jubilee Ball he was seen dancing with the daughter of the Duchess of Roxburgh!

Something had to be done. Curzon countered by issuing a directive that Indian princes would only be allowed to visit Europe for special reasons. When he had to consider which princes to send to London to attend the coronation of Edward VII in 1901, he selected those of dignified appearance and traditional manners. The Rajah of Nabha was 'a very fine and noble-looking man', and the Maharajah of Jaipur was 'a distinguished-looking man, rather heavy and fat, but of eminently dignified and impressive appearance'. Only the most 'civilized' princes were chosen to represent their country.

But there was another difficulty. Despite the governing idea of white women being at risk from lascivious Indians, the problem arose of white women in England running after the Indians in the princes' entourage. Curzon felt it incumbent upon him to warn the Secretary of State, Lord Hamilton, of this risk: 'The woman aspect of the question is rather difficult, since strange as it may seem English women of the housemaid class, and even higher, do offer themselves to these Indian soldiers, attracted by their uniform, enamoured of their physique, and with a sort of idea that the warrior is also an oriental prince.'

Later, Hamilton was able to reassure Curzon that the Indians, at least, behaved 'with all restraint and propriety . . . making allowance for all the temptations to which they were subject', for Hamilton had indeed detected 'a very unpleasant characteristic . . . . the craze of white women for running after black men.' Curzon, however, knew that once back in India the princes and their trains would 'fall very quickly back into their proper place'.

There was the threat of homosexuality too (described by Hamilton as 'the special oriental vice'). Curzon had founded a Cadet Corps for young Indian princelings, and to it he sent one young ruler to cure him of homosexual leanings. He then promptly became nervous that the boy would 'corrupt' the other cadets. But the fear of homosexuality paled in importance beside the Threat to the White Woman: that the white woman herself plainly didn't find Indians repellent presented a problem: such an idea was a threat to the white man and the trigger for jealousy. The Indian had to be presented as someone to be avoided.

Often he could not help but look unappealing – he lived in poverty and squalor which his enlightened rulers did nothing to relieve. Frances Shebbeare remembers how it was in Karachi, where her father was Governor in the 1930s:

> I had a little car of my own. And a rather alarming thing you could do sometimes was to go down to the bazaar, to the Indian shops, because people said, 'oh, you can get things much cheaper there'. I remember going a couple of times. I didn't like it at all. It was very uncomfortable. They had little tiny alleyways of streets, and everybody was crowding in on them. They weren't going to hit you or steal, really, but it was just rather frightening. One hardly ever did it. If you wanted anything from the bazaar, you sent your bearer. I just remember all these terribly poor people, all crowding up around you. One couldn't have gone in one's car. And of course at that time Karachi was tiny.

The crowds are something which harass the European to this day. Even in the relatively peaceful haven of Simla it was not very different, though Frances Shebbeare was there after the order banning Indians from The Mall (keeping it exclusively 'for whites only') had been rescinded. The present-day traveller to Simla cannot help but be struck by the sheer Englishness of Christ Church, a masterpiece of suburban Gothic inside and out – a little bit of Surrey in an alien land. 'The memsahibs created a replica of life back home,' observes former Indian diplomat Pran Nevill. But in the Indian town, as Frances Shebbeare recalls:

> There was a top road there which you used if you wanted to get from one side of the town to the other. I used to use the bottom road if I was riding, but I wouldn't have gone there on my feet, not for anything. It was full of people crowded together, roasting corncobs, and there were horrible smells. It was the crowdedness I disliked. We lived in a kind of refined, rarefied atmosphere up at the top. It was awful really – but perhaps it wasn't. Look at all the jobs we gave to everybody. Every horse probably supported a family.

A Woman's Place

❧§❧

To pass the time, there was tennis, there was bridge, and there was intrigue. The hill stations were the place for that, as grass widows spent the warm season there, going to dances with officers on leave. Even so, 'you lived in a goldfish bowl,' as Kit Mullan remembers from her time in Assam.

> There was a Mrs Hauksbee type at Shillong. She had an unfortunate husband labouring somewhere or other, but he didn't

turn up often. She wasn't produced socially at all, she just lived her own life, and that is probably the way she wanted it. She had her own clientele, and in the end she probably retired quite well off and went to live an exemplary existence of boredom in Brighton, or somewhere . . . . Occasionally there'd be a domestic dust-up, and somebody would have an affair, just from sheer boredom, and then you'd find the chap would be sent off to cool his heels in the worst possible district in the province, and she'd be sent home to cool *her* heels with Mother in Eastbourne, and be dusted down by her. But after a couple of months she'd arrive back, with new clothes and looking as if butter wouldn't melt in her mouth, and all was forgiven and forgotten. A much better way of doing it, I think, than this divorce and splitting up of children and all the rest of it that goes on now.

Was it easier for working-class Englishwomen? They certainly weren't quite so trapped in the drawing-room conventions of home. Dorothy Steel went out to India in the late 1920s following her marriage to a drum major. She set out from Tilbury on the ss *Rampura* and arrived in Bombay six weeks later. 'There were thirty of us just married going out and another forty going out to get married because they'd sent their pictures but when they got there three blokes refused to marry their girls because they'd sent the wrong pictures.

'I got there and I was homesick, and I thought I'm not going to stay. But then when I had such a nice husband who looked after me, well, then I did stay, I stayed ten years.' She thought Bombay was dreadful, though, and that was before she knew about the four-day train journey she faced with her husband to get to his barracks at Secunderabad. 'But he had arranged that we had a nice dinner; but I said "well, I don't think I'm going to like food cooked by black people." "Oh," he says, "you will. It'll be lovely."'

She soon came round to India: 'It's nice isn't it when you're in love and there's the lovely smell of acacia trees and the flame of the forest trees, and you know I thought it was rather lovely actually, and I had lovely silk underclothes.' Her husband, Arthur, warned her to keep herself shut in when he was away. 'I didn't know a word of Hindustani. He said, "you must keep the door shut . . . the cook will get the rations and so on." Well, there came a big knock on the door and it was the *beestie* [water carrier], and he called out, "Memsahib, memsahib," and one or two others congregated as I wouldn't let them in but in the end he shouted out, "Memsahib, shit pot empty." Well, I thought it was dreadful, but that must have been the only English that he knew. He wanted to empty the commode.'

> 🙶 'There were only ten girls in the barracks and only three sergeants' wives. Very few officers' wives – they had lots of money in those days and they used to come out and then go back every few months. I learnt to play tennis and I smoked but I could never get to like gin and tonic.'

Because there were so few women, Dorothy's husband Arthur drew up a few ground rules:

He said, 'There are a thousand troops here and they would all like to have a bit of fun with you, but I do not want that. If you have fun with these boys I'll send you home.' And I said, 'well, you're quite safe there because I won't'; but it was fun really because he didn't dance and I did and we used to go to dances and I used to get mobbed. I never did anything naughty but I had lots of lovely love letters. I was horrified of course and I tore them up because I didn't want my husband to see them, but really I wish I'd kept them now because they were so lovely, and it just went on.

Dorothy would play tennis and bridge with Indians, but didn't like to dance with them. She disliked the way her husband treated them: 'He never said please or thank you. I don't think he was nice to them, but nobody was; still, he was nicer than most. When we left India we didn't owe a penny and the cook came everywhere with us and he said, "Please, sahib, please take me home". We'd had him for ten years. He was really heartbroken.'

There wasn't always a lot that women who had married into British Indian society could *do*. After she had married her tea planter, Iris MacFarlane went to live in Assam:

When the children went home [to England] I was left to my own resources, and then I really started looking round. I thought, well, I've got another fifteen years here, what am I going to do with them? What is this place I'm living in? And then things began to emerge in a clearer light. I shook the bars of my cage quite violently, but never got out of it. Because my role was just to be subservient and fit into the system, and if I had been unpleasant or insisted on my rights, I don't think my husband would have been able to stay there. That was the problem. It was very much a man's world.

She did her best. She learnt the language. She started a family plan-
ning clinic – which was unpopular with the hospital board because
they wanted the locals to breed and provide cheap labour for the
plantations. The board also refused to spend money flyproofing the
hospital. She taught in the school, and brought one peasant boy to
the point where he was about to sit his matriculation examination.
But then he cheeked a local babu's daughter and was expelled. Iris
resigned in protest. 'In the end I made myself very unhappy and
finally very ill. And I don't think I achieved anything. Whereas the
other women out there really liked it. They enjoyed the life and
they never felt the frustration that I felt at all.'

The situation of British women in India continued to be a cause
of much anxiety. Iris MacFarlane also points out that 'the men were
very suspicious of their women moving out of their particular
groove or out of their particular role. A woman's place was assigned
to her and she had to stay in it; and somehow she was a threat to the
whole society if she moved out of it. She would be questioning the
men's values, I suppose, if she did.' And yet some women were
regarded with something approaching scorn by the very men who
professed to be their protectors. Perhaps it all had more to do with
the schoolboyish attitude to women for which Englishmen are notorious. Tom Collins remembers the attitude he and his brother
officers had towards the 'fishing fleet': 'If you got mixed up with the
fishing fleet it was a joke. You didn't go playing around with them.
If you went to a dance you danced with a different girl every time.
If you fell in love you got teased.' Ruper Mayne, in India in the
1930s, says, 'I think my wife [whom he met in India] would be very
angry if I called her "fishing fleet".' Colonel Wallace Pryke, how-

❦ Colonel Guyan Dubey recollects that as a young Indian officer in the early 1930s he joined the Dacca Club. It had a swimming-pool, but the day after he'd used it for the first time, he was told not to do so again – 'I was told that I shouldn't see British women in swimming costumes – "it's not done" – or words to that effect. I felt very sore and sad. I said, "why not? I am not misbehaving with the girls; I am not doing anything that I should not do."' His wife remembers how an uncle of hers, rejected by a white girl on grounds of race, went off to the Foreign Legion for five years. She also remembers how, as a young Indian army wife, she had to endure the condescension of the wives of her husband's white brother officers.

ever, remembers how difficult it was for a young officer to meet girls, and that the girls who came over from England were 'very, very popular'.

Social Codes and Censure

❦❧❦

At first, people posted to Africa left their wives at home. 'What would a white woman in the interior of Africa have done all day? I mean she would have cut her throat,' points out Henrietta Fanshawe who lived in the Gold Coast in the 1920s. But as the Empire spread, nervousness about white women in this strange and different land was transformed into a powerful social code, as the daughter of a white settler in Kenya, Jane Elliot, recalls:

> One was always very careful. One would never have left one's children alone with them. Certainly not if they were girls, because that was supposed to be a temptation to them. My husband [a police officer] was terribly careful. He never would let any servant of ours come into our bedroom. In fact I always had to make my own bed; he never would allow them to do anything like that for me. It was just a feeling of what was right and proper: that you didn't do certain things.
>
> My husband's point of view was that the white women, and there weren't all that many of them, who did get themselves raped were asking for it. Some of the women used to walk about in the house when their servants were doing the cleaning, washing, or cooking, or whatever, dressed in a nightie or a pair of shorts, or a bath towel half draped around them, or even just in their skin. Those were the sort of people who got raped. It wasn't fair on the African to behave like that. My husband was very pro-African at the time when it wasn't necessarily done to be pro-African, but he knew that there was a certain way you had to behave. He was terribly firm with my daughters and me, to make sure that we never did anything that might arouse – or possibly disgust – the African. You couldn't let yourself down. You were white, and you had to behave decently. My husband set a very high standard.

Fear was not something that necessarily played a role in the white woman's life, as Kit Mullan recollects of her time growing up in Nyasaland:

> My father would be away all day, and anybody could have had us in that time, and the house was a couple of miles from

Blantyre. But my mother used to go out, and wander round the place, and visit friends. She had her own rickshaw, and she used to go off to the Scottish Mission, for example. But there was no sense of fear in being alone. If my father had to go off on circuit, you'd have a night guard with a lantern, and he'd wrap himself in a blanket and sleep on the verandah. He was supposed to rescue you if anything went wrong, but as there were no telephones. I don't know what he'd have done. But nothing ever happened.

Danger – real or imagined – wasn't always from the locals. In the Gold Coast, Henrietta Fanshawe was pursued by a lovelorn police officer called John Massey for sometime. She was never very keen, but the crunch came one day when she went to meet him at the station in Mentoni: 'He was wearing a pink flannel shirt, which I disapproved of passionately, and he was swearing at the porters because his whisky hadn't been delivered. This was too much for me so I rushed home and I said to Mother – "I wouldn't marry John Massey if he was the last man on earth."'

Betty Matthews had a rather different experience. In 1947, soon after leaving Cambridge, she married her first husband, who'd been a friend for some time, travelling out with him that same year to Port Herald, Nyasaland, where he was District Commissioner. His work kept him hugely busy and he was away for much of the time, so she spent a lot of time alone at the Residency. 'The roof was full of bats, and at night we used to stand on the verandah and watch them take off. The roof was also full of guano, and I could never smell it afterwards without feeling nostalgic. We had a tin hip-bath, and a thunder-box lavatory with a pressure lamp which used to throw the shadows of the spiders and the insects onto the walls as you sat enthroned.' Later, the Residency was taken over by ants and they had to decamp to the guest house next door.

It wasn't a bad life at first, and Betty learnt Bantu from the cook's wife. But after six months or so her increasingly silent husband informed her that things weren't working out between them and that he would prefer to take an African wife:

> I think the marriage broke down because I wasn't the person my husband thought I was . . . . He told me he'd thought I was more like a man than a woman, sort of mentally, and that when he was out on station I would be a companion for him on his own level of thinking, those were his words, and that if he was unhappy and wished to have an African wife I would not object because it seemed reasonable . . . but I wanted a nice house and to bother about the furniture and the decorating, and I wanted to make a nice, pretty garden, and that kind of thing didn't interest him in the least.
>
> I became very upset, and we argued about it, and I went up into the hills and tried to behave like an African woman, learning how to plaster mud on walls and that kind of thing, but it didn't work.

Apart from anything else, her African servants wouldn't let her do any real work. In the end the fatherly Provincial Commissioner, on a visit, noticed how unhappy she was, and rescued her by taking her down to Blantyre with him, where she shared a house with his secretary. Her husband was perfectly happy with this arrangement. 'I saw him a couple of months later and he told me he'd married an African woman by local law and custom . . . and that was the end of it . . . . I think he really loved the Africans, and preferred their company to anyone else's, but his native marriage contravened some sort of government regulation. The Provincial Commissioner told me that if it ever became public he would have to take action and my husband would have to resign. But the code was very narrow then, even for Europeans. I knew of another District Commissioner who was ordered to marry the white woman he was living with or leave his post.' The locals had their own codes of censure. Betty Matthews remembers a local chief who expressed his disapproval of a colonial governor by leaving out his false teeth when summoned to a meeting; and much later on, after she had remarried, her own cook was furious when she allowed his children to share some cakes he'd cooked for her family.

Crime and Punishment

◦§§◦

A crucial event in the development of concern about women was what became one of the epics of the British Empire. Indians call it the Great Rebellion; the British called it the Indian Mutiny.

Whatever the underlying reasons for the Mutiny were, it was sparked by the issue to the Army of a new Enfield rifle, which used greased cartridges that had to be bitten open to release their powder. Early in 1857 a rumour circulated among the sepoy companies in Bengal that the grease contained elements of beef and pork fat, the one offensive to Hindus and the other to Moslems. It was seen as a deliberate ploy to undermine Indian religious tradition. Isolated incidents snowballed into a full but inchoate rebellion which centred loosely on the elderly and powerless last Mogul emperor, Bahadur Shah Zafar, in Delhi. It spread fast and furiously and threatened the continuation of British power in India. If it had been focused it might have succeeded. In the event it was put down relatively quickly; but two events cast permanent shadows on the path of history – the siege and relief of Lucknow, and the massacre at Kanpur.

Whereas Bahadur was a Moslem figurehead, the Hindu revolt centred on the last of the Mahratta kings, Nana Sahib, an indolent middle-aged man who lived in the palm of the British hand, in his palace not far from the town of Kanpur.

In 1857 the British garrison under Sir Hugh Wheeler withdrew into makeshift defences as the rebel army approached and besieged the city, taking with them the European civilian population. At first Nana Sahib offered to aid them, but soon took sides with the enemy. After a long siege and many fatalities, a peace was negotiated and the British were offered free passage down the Ganges to safety. But no sooner had they embarked, having handed over their weapons, than Nana Sahib gave the order to fire. The slaughter was tremendous – only four men escaped by chance. The surviving women and children were taken to a house in Kanpur and butchered to death there a month later.

The relieving British troops under Brigadier-General James Neill were appalled, and took swift and savage reprisals. Rebels were made to lick the blood of the slaughtered victims from the mud walls of the house where the women and children had been slaughtered. A common form of execution used was to lash offenders across the barrels of cannon – 'you heard the roar of the guns, and above the smoke you saw legs, arms and heads blown in all directions. Since that time we have had an execution parade once or twice a week, and such is the force of habit we now think little of them.' But the British reaction was not as intemperate as it might have been, and an argument ran that to blow people from guns afforded the victim an instantaneous and therefore relatively humane death, while at the same time providing an adequately deterrent spectacle.

Lucknow had been annexed by the Raj as late as 1856. In the year of the Mutiny, the province of Oudh was quickly overrun until only the city remained in British hands. In June, the community withdrew into the Residency compound, which was garrisoned and prepared for a siege. And a siege there was – it lasted over ninety days until relief came to the beleaguered people within. Throughout they had striven to maintain correct standards of behaviour in the face of threatening death and starvation. But the relief was a false dawn: the already exhausted relieving column was itself besieged, and the additional numbers meant that food was in even shorter supply than ever. People were reduced to eating sparrows, chloroform had run out so that surgical operations had to be performed without it, and disease was rife among the howitzer-blasted buildings. It was not until towards the end of November that a second relieving force was finally able to rescue the survivors.

Still, the British were not innocent of atrocities as the Mutiny was put down and, as the chronicler of the British Empire James Morris notes in *Heaven's Command*, 'far from weakening the imperial confidence of the British, on a conscious level at least the Mutiny hardened and coarsened it. It brought out the worst in many of them. Even the heroines of the Lucknow siege, when they were relieved at last, came stumbling out with bags of rupees in their arms, and did nothing but grumble . . . .' No shrinking violets there, apparently.

At home, the hysterical press trumpeted outrage: 'every tree and gable-end in the place [India] should have its burden in the shape of a mutineer's carcass,' yelped *The Times*. The British never forgot the experience. At Kanpur they erected a monument to their dead, and it became one of the places of pilgrimage of the Raj. In Lucknow, the Residency building, where the British had held out, was left in ruins, surrounded by ornate Victorian memorials.

The official tendency, however, was towards a more liberal administration, acknowledging that Indians must be given more say, however gradually, in the management of their country. But this was in the main a London view, not shared by Calcutta, especially with regard to what had become one of the central, or centrally symbolic issues, of maintenance of power: the need to protect the women. In February 1883, Courtenay Peregrine Ilbert, the law member of liberal Viceroy Lord Ripon's executive council, introduced a Bill to amend the code of criminal procedure in the Indian Penal Code. In effect, the Ilbert Bill was designed to allow white people to be tried by Indian judges anywhere in British India.

Reaction was instantaneous, and the memsahibs played no passive role. Various fears stimulated it: that Indian judges might be polygynous; that they might use their power sexually to harass English servant girls they coveted; that their ideas would be affected by their perception of their own women, who were 'low and coarse'; that they might be favourably disposed towards Indian rapists. Behind it all was a general fear of any increase in the power of Indian officials.

Mrs J. F. Norris, the wife of an English judge not noted for his liberal views on the question of race, got up a huge movement against the Bill, and in the 'anti' camp were to be found even such progressive people as Annette Beveridge, who wrote about 'Mr Ilbert's proposal to subject civilised women to the jurisdiction of men who have done little or nothing to redeem the women of their own races, and whose social ideas are still on the outer verges of civilisation.' The shrinking violet reappeared, this time weeping in the dock, at the mercy of mocking and exultant natives:

> Tell him each man among us
> Would lavish forth his life,
> The father for his daughter,
> The husband for his wife;
> Ere these poor Christian women
> To glut some menial's grudge,
> Stand in the dock, the aliens' mock,
> Before an alien judge.

The heavily emotional Victorian language once again concealed unsavoury truths. In mid-1883 in Calcutta, Mrs James Hume, the wife of a prosecuting counsel, was apparently raped by her sweeper, Hurroo Mehta. Her husband had found them together in the bathroom and thrashed the man forthwith. The case was rushed through the courts and Mehta was sentenced to eight years' rigorous punishment. But he was innocent. Mrs Hume had been having an affair with him for six months. To protect her name, the couple had agreed to perjure themselves, as Hume confessed to the Viceroy, Lord Dufferin, two years later.

As Dr David Anderson of the School of African and Oriental Studies remarks, 'At times of political crisis or of economic downturn, or when a particular incident of a sexual nature perhaps might occur, matters might conspire to provoke a heightening of anxiety,

RIGHT 12 Frances Shebbeare dressed for a garden party at the Viceregal Lodge, Delhi, in 1935.
BELOW 13 Iris MacFarlane (right) with her sisters. Despite coming from a family that had been involved with the Raj for generations, as a married woman Iris found the restricted life frustrating.

BELOW 14 Kit Mullan's parents at Blantyre, Nyasaland, in 1901. The Mullans did not succumb to the usual colonial paranoia about female vulnerability and Kit recalls being left at home with her mother whilst her father was away.

ABOVE
15 At the hill stations in India the
memsahibs re-created a society identical to
the one they had left in England –
complete with a Mall to parade along.

LEFT
16 Rule Britannia: the cover of *The
Imperial Colonist* magazine in 1905,
published by the British Women's
Emigration Association.

ABOVE
17 The popular image of the
settler: 'Moffatt, erect and
fearless, threw open his waistcoat
and cried, "Now, if you will,
strike your spears into my
heart!"' (from *Heroes of
Britain in Peace and War*.)

RIGHT
18 An article reporting the
Grogan affair in *The East African
Standard*, 16 March 1907.

THE CLIMAX.

Natives publicly Flogged by President of Colonists' Association.

THE COURT HOUSE THE SCENE.

Are European Ladies to be insulted by Natives?

(PRESS TELEGRAM.)
Nairobi, Thursday.
Mr. E. S. Grogan, President of the
Colonists' Associaton and visiting

and then the undercurrent wells up into a kind of tidal wave of much wider anxiety, a form almost of hysteria.'

The 'Back Peril'

❧❦❧

Elsewhere in the Empire, and especially where British people aimed to settle, the 'Black Peril', as it was called, became a staple element of settler politics. In 1907, Nairobi was still a frontier town. The European settlers were having difficulty setting up their farms. Africans were unwilling to work on them, and relations between the settlers and the government were poor. The settler Ewart Grogan was President of the Colonists' Association at this time. He was a man of strong feeling and actions. He was very able, but also intensely vain. In a book describing his trek from the Cape to Cairo, he described a meeting with a recalcitrant African chieftan: '. . . things reached a climax, the chief telling me that he wanted no white men in his country, that the Portuguese forced them to work for nothing, and demanded a 5 rupee hut tax, that my men would obtain no food, etc, etc. *ad nauseam*. In thirty seconds he was prone, and taking a severe dose of hippo-whip before his astonished band of elders; he rose refreshed and brought me flour and fowls, guides to show me game, and a guide to Chiperoni for the morrow . . . .'

The colonists were increasingly angry at the government's liberal attitude towards the Kikuyu – not just on account of land grants, but over the government's refusal to encourage Africans to work on white farms, for without cheap labour they would have been hard to run at a profit. In the difficult atmosphere of the early 1900s, an event occurred which enabled Grogan to up the ante. His daughter, Jane Elliot, remembers;

> I think it was my mother and her sister-in-law – my father's eldest sister – who were trying to take a couple of rickshaws from the centre of Nairobi to go back to their houses in Muthaiga, and my rather tiresome aunt obviously said something that upset a rickshaw boy and he let go of his handles, with the result that my aunt was thrown out of the rickshaw backwards, and of course in those days that was an absolutely unthinkable thing to do. The boy was duly reported to my father and I think he gave him a very minor punishment, two or three chunks with a whip, and that was that.

But apparently that was not that. Grogan took his *kiboko* – his hippo-whip – and went in search of the boys. Apparently there had been three boys, not two, and they were drunk. Apparently both women were in the same rickshaw. Grogan's biographer reports: 'with frightening yells and much laughter the puller threw the shafts of the rickshaw up in the air and the women bounced up and down as the rickshaw hit the ground to the delight of the other two . . . .' The women screamed and asked the boys to let them off; they were pulled roughly clear of the rickshaw and left to walk the rest of the way home. To make matters worse, it appears that the boys may actually have been in Grogan's employ.

Grogan didn't quite go into action the minute he heard about the outrage. He consulted his friend, the Vice-President of the Colonists' Association, Sydney Fichat, who advised him to sleep on it. He did, but awoke with his anger unabated. He located the boys and took them forcibly into Nairobi, marching them to the town magistrate's court. There the magistrate, E. R. Logan, remonstrated with him, but Grogan expressed himself sceptical of the efficacy of official justice. By now a sympathetic crowd had gathered. With two other white men, Bowker and Gray, Grogan now gave the three Africans twenty-five lashes each, before letting them go and retiring to his club for a drink.

He was not allowed to get away with it, but his trial revealed just how much support he enjoyed from the white settler community. In court he said, 'I look upon any matter connected with the safety of my womenfolk as so important that I do not consider it justified, as a family man, to leave it to the vagaries of the law and the application thereof, and I wish the natives to understand, and it should be generally understood, that any action of that sort involves a far greater risk than "horsetooth mealie" (prison food).' The *East African Standard* commented: 'Captain Grogan was undoubtedly justified in using physical force as the provocation was of a kind no man will brook . . . . Grogan was sentenced to two months' imprisonment, which he served in some style in a house on the hill above Nairobi, according to his own account being served cake every day by the grateful white women of the town.

Jane Elliot, who is by no means uncritical of her father, finds the whole episode – which occurred before she was born – incredible, 'it doesn't sound like my father at all'. She adds that use of the whip was rare among the settlers and anyone who did use it was ostracized by his peers. However, the incident did Grogan's career in Kenyan politics no harm. The debates in the newspapers went into great detail about how at risk settler women were on lonely farms, and how vulnerable women were walking the streets of Nairobi.

Soon afterwards, Kenya got its own Legislative Council, but Grogan's name was left off its list of members. Nevertheless, when the East African protectorate became the Kenya Colony, and regional electorates were set up for the Legislative Council, Grogan became a long-serving member, and a thorn in the side of the administration: 'I think my father was a very political animal. He thought everybody else was a fool and generally said so, which of course didn't endear him very much to government; but I think the settlers went along with him quite well because he did speak for them, and we did have a point – which most people never acknowledged, of course.'

The 'Black Peril' myth persisted, fuelled in Kenya by a number of incidents. In 1920, between March and May, four cases of child assault came before the courts in Nairobi. These cases generated a huge panic among the settler community, who feared that they represented an epidemic of child abuse by Africans against European children, and the paranoia was fuelled by the press.

> ≈ The Legislative Assembly set up a commission of enquiry, which reported that from 1910 to 1920 there had only been sixteen cases of sexual assault against Europeans, and of those only one was the rape of an adult woman. Seven were against children, and these were in every case committed by African boys aged between ten and fifteen, employed as servants in European households. The age of the victims was between two and seven, and what particularly outraged the settlers was that in some cases the children had contracted venereal disease.

The settlers knew little about local sexual behaviour. As we have seen, African males were thought to be creatures of unbridled lust. Black women, too, were held to be highly libidinous. There was also a belief that Africans thought a sure cure for VD was to have sexual intercourse with a virgin, and preferably a virgin child. This belief among the whites was propagated by the East African Women's League.

It was not valid. In fact there is evidence to show that it may originally have been a European superstition. But the scare was enough for settlers to demand the death penalty for anyone who assaulted European women and children. This demand met with no success in 1920, but the issue came up again six years later when a seventy-year-old woman, a Mrs Ulyate, was raped and knifed during a robbery at her isolated farmstead at Kijabe, to the west of Nairobi.

The Ulyates were a prominent settler family of Boer extraction, and Mrs Ulyate, who survived her ordeal, went public about it. This was enough to effect the passing of a law authorizing the death penalty for rape by a black of a white. Similar laws came to be passed elsewhere in the Empire, from South Africa to New Guinea. But the anxiety concerning white children continued. Dr Keith Batten encountered it as a doctor in Kampala, Uganda, in the 1950s:

> There were only a very few cases, but as so often with these things you've only got to have one case in a community, and everyone's worried that the next victim might be their child. Certain tribes had a belief that one way of curing venereal disease was to have intercourse with a virgin, and in their terms that meant a child of seven or eight. One European child was brought into our hospital suffering from gonorrhoea, a small

child of six or seven. It'd obviously been interfered with and this was pointed out to the mother. It was immediately assumed that the culprit must have been one of the African staff who'd been looking after her. It would never have occurred to any of us that a European could have done such a thing.

Batten's own wife had a frightening encounter with one of their servants some time after this incident, though the young man turned out to be mentally unstable and the couple did not prosecute.

Rape of the Ruled

The sense of danger involved in Empire cut both ways. Just as Europeans believed that their women were in danger, so did their subjects, and perhaps with more justification.

Today, Taramoni Dasi lives in Calcutta, but as a child she lived in a Bengali village, and remembers the fear engendered by the arrival of imperial forces during the time of the salt protest of 1930. The aim of Gandhi and the Indian Congress was to protest against the government monopoly and tax on the manufacture of salt. Away from the publicity of Gandhi's famous march to the sea at Dandi in Gujerat, the villagers feared for their women as the government enforced the law: 'At Mondirer bazaar there was a warning to vacate the market because the sahib soldiers were coming. At the time, our cooking was in progress. I was in the bazaar with my brother and my father. It was a very busy day. There was no boundary round our house, so we had to run away. All the wives and maidservants fled away to somebody else's house and kept the door shut. The rumour was that the soldiers were going to grab the women.'

The British in fact made strenuous efforts to keep the Army, and particularly the British troops, away from the native population precisely to avoid rapes. But it was impossible to be vigilant all the time. Harry Bowen was a sixteen-year-old trumpeter in the Royal Artillery stationed at Kanpur in 1930:

> There was one time I remember that an Indian woman strayed into the lines where we were barracked, and she got into very serious trouble. I don't know whether she'd come in by mistake or whether she was looking for business, but things must've got out of hand and she was passed from bed to bed and finished up as a dead body on the incinerator in the morning . . . . There'd been about twenty-four to thirty fellows involved, probably a lot more than that. She couldn't take it. It killed her.
>
> Of course the police came and they questioned a lot of people, but they couldn't pin it on any one person, so the whole thing petered out. We thought it was pretty disgusting; it let the unit down. That's all. The thing was she had come in of her own accord and that was the result. It wasn't a question of anybody else being involved. She just appeared in the confines of the unit and that was it.

Under the law of India, barracks or cantonment areas were under military rather than the civil administration. Yardonath Singh, who was active in the independence movement in Kanpur, remembers the concern that this caused:

> Near Company Park there was a military post. They were all Englishmen there. Once they abducted two Indian women who went up to the park to bathe. They took them into the jungle and after they'd molested them they strangled them. They

found the bodies the next day. And the women who cut the grass near the aerodrome weren't safe, either. But no one was allowed to interfere. It was all up to the colonel and the brigadier. They were in charge. If there were court-martials, they were held in camera. The public didn't know what they were doing.

One thing is certain though – the mistreatment of women contributed to the cause of independence. It created hatred in the hearts of Indians who heard about it. It was one of the things which helped the movement to drive the Britishers out of India.

4

⋟⋞

Paying the Price

Madam Life's a piece in bloom
Death goes dogging everywhere;
She's the tenant of the room,
He's the ruffian on the stair.

To W. R.
W. E. Henley (1849 – 1903)

Whores were part and parcel of the Empire. For most of the nineteenth century, a battle raged between the practicalities of satisfying the sexual desires of an army of colonial men and the outraged sensibilities of those at home who heard vile stories of brothels, harlotry and vice from the Empire. Donal McKenna, who took to the seafaring life as a young man after the Second World War, to see the world and escape the dreariness of dockland Dublin, recalls the kind of ritual encountered in a Bombay brothel in the 1950s: 'The madam would greet you and ask you if you wanted a short time, or any fetishes, but mainly it was just a short time you wanted. And they would show you into a small room and there might be one or two girls, and you would make your choice and go off to another small room with a bed, and there would always be a light on the side, and some of the girls would put the light behind your penis and have a look. What they hoped to find I don't know, but they would inspect you before intercourse took place.' The chances are that the girls were looking for traces of disease.

In India in the 1930s Medical Officer Dr John Sarkies remembers how the young troops would set off for the red light district: 'Transport was arranged for them to go down, and there would always be touts who would pick them up in the street and say, "You want a nice girl, I'll show you," and off the unfortunate British soldier would be led and in due course he would appear on sick parade with either syphilis or gonorrhoea.'

Settlers, planters, members of the Civil Service and businessmen who worked and lived in the Empire were, at least theoretically, able to maintain the high standards of sexual probity required by the self-imposed code of conduct of the British for the simple reason that they were at perfect liberty to marry. If one excepts the senior officer class, the same was not true of soldiers. By 1871 30 per cent of officers were married, but of those under the age of twenty-four, only two per cent had wives. The broad rule was, 'subalterns cannot marry, captains may marry, majors should marry, colonels must marry.'

The Army, however, understood the need a man had to indulge his natural urges, and it was also felt that special provision should be made for British Other Ranks in this respect, because they were working-class, and were thus deemed to be wanting in the moral and material resources required for marriage, except for those very few who were permitted to marry 'on the strength' of a regiment, and who were granted married quarters. Attractive young wives on station were very much the centre of attention, even riskily so.

From the 1830s on, at least, as the historian Kenneth Ballhatchet points out, the British 'official élite ... were supposed to shun Indian mistresses and content themselves with British wives, for rulers should be aloof from the people and so trusted as beyond corruption and feared as remote from the ways of the common man. The prestige of the ruling race came to be a matter for serious concern.' By 1901, there were 170 000 Europeans in India, ruling 294 million Indians and 89 000 Anglo-Indians.

Chaste Crusaders and Their Adversaries

🙠🙠

The situation was not helped by the popular rise of the Moral Guardian – a self-appointed sexual purity policeman (or woman) who rose in prominence in the nineteenth century on the back of the narrow-minded Evangelical Movement of the late eighteenth century. Of course they were not all bad people, and not all of them were motivated by prurience, but an unfortunately large number of them *were*, and others were misguided, and from these two types did the most vociferous examples come.

The members of the various Purity movements impeded what might otherwise have been a satisfactory way of controlling prostitution – a profession which in any case it is impossible to stamp out, and which in the context of the time was very necessary. What was the average British soldier to do? He couldn't have a native mistress, masturbation was considered injurious to health, and homosexuality was regarded with total horror and revulsion. The Army couldn't occupy all of every day with cold baths and exercise. For a lot of the time soldiers were forbidden to be in the open air, for fear

of the sun. There was a limit to the entertainment playing cards
could provide, and although allowances of drink were wildly generous – a gallon of spirits every twenty days, a quart of strong beer
and two drams of rum a day – an alcoholic soldier would pretty soon
find himself in the guardhouse or out of a job altogether.
Nevertheless alcoholism was a severe problem in the Army at the
time.

There were other very simple practical difficulties to be overcome
if prostitution was to be avoided: 'Of course, marriage would be a
better remedy,' pointed out the reforming Indian Civil Servant C. E.
Trevelyan – a brother-in-law of Lord Macaulay – 'but where were
wives to be found for successive relays of 70 000 men?' Indian
troops did not have the same problem: most of them were older, and
there were no marriage restrictions upon them. The married quarters provided for them were very basic, but they did exist. And, as
Lieutenant-Colonel Sharma of the Indian Army indicates:

> The Indian soldier is a very god-fearing person, and he won't
> go and get another girl out of his caste; also he was given two
> months' leave every year to go back home, so his requirements
> from that side were met, but the British soldier was away for a
> long time from his people, from his family, and so for him
> there was a requirement to meet his needs in spite of all the
> control he would get . . . . I am sure a British soldier is as god-
> fearing as an Indian; probably in his own home in England I'm
> sure he would behave better than he behaves when he's outside
> in the colonial army or fighting a war.

Sexual repression in society means good business for porno-
graphers and prostitutes, and although people in the nineteenth
century didn't *talk* about sex as much as we do now, of course their
sexual appetites were just the same. In 1889 the homosexual
scandals of the gay brothel in Cleveland Street, London, which
catered to some of the highest in the land, and that surrounding
Oscar Wilde's trial a decade or so later, showed that even the 'Love
That Dared Not Speak Its Name' was alive and well and very healthy
in Victorian England; and what went for Victorian England, went
for the Empire. A certain Captain Kenneth Searight, whom E. M.
Forster met on the voyage out in 1912, celebrated his conquests in a
wittily written poem in rhyming couplets, of which the following
short extract is a very mild example:

> *And now the scene shifted and I passed*
> *From sensuous Bengal to fierce Peshawar*
> *As Asiatic stronghold where each flower*
> *Of boyhood planted in its restless soil*
> *Is – ipso facto – ready to despoil*
> *(Or be despoiled by) someone else; the yarn*
> *Indeed so has it that the young Pathan*
> *Thinks it peculiar if you would pass*
> *Him by without some reference to his arse.*

> ৪৯ Prostitution was a condition of the Empire. The British takeover and development of two-thirds of the globe was accomplished by a huge influx of men, most of them single. Thousand upon thousand of them came to build, fight, mine, trade and extract profits from the new territories. In their wake came a massive expansion of prostitution on an international scale that matched the Empire itself. Thousands of women were moved all over the globe, as organized consortia of pimps utilized the new railways and shipping lines to move their product to where there was a demand for it. The need for a common language, essential in any courtship, was circumvented by prostitution.

White Slaves?

◆§৪৯

In India, as we have seen, prostitution was an honourable and age-old profession. From Free School Street in Calcutta to Cursetji Sukhlaji Street in Bombay, the red light districts were as established and recognized as, say, Inns of Court. Although admittedly in Calcutta the brothel 'district' was uncontrollable – the more so because of the large number of white low-lifers and discharged sailors among the poor in the town – in Bombay it was successfully confined to the area it still occupies around Kamathipura. 'I've been outside the Free School,' remembers Lieutentant-Colonel Sharma. 'I've never been inside one, but they were good localities, good areas, good houses at that time – that was during the war; I don't know what they are like now. One would go inside and talk to the girls nicely – they could speak English, and there would be Eurasian girls and girls from all sorts of different countries. But they would be good places, not like outside the cantonments.'

There were plenty of European prostitutes in Bombay, of whom a large proportion were Russian and East European Jewesses fleeing persecution in their own countries. There were also several Arabian Jewish girls, and Japanese girls – Japanese prostitutes having the reputation for being the cleanest, best mannered, and most accomplished in the art of love-making.

The European girls were organized by a system of 'white slavery', though it seems that not all the girls by any means went unwillingly. A case in point was that of Fanny Epstein, born in Poland but living with her parents in London when she disappeared in 1891 aged eighteen, having recently met a handsome thirty-four-year-old, Alexander Kahn. Her father, with the aid of the National Vigilance Association – one of the Purity organizations – finally tracked her down to Bombay, where she was living with a friend who had left London at the same time, Annie Gould. Interviewed by the police, she denied any coercion, seemed perfectly happy, refused to go home, and continued to run the saloon bar where she had been discovered. The National Vigilance Association meanwhile brought an unsuccessful action against Kahn for the abduction of a minor (no one could prove that he had actually *abducted* her), and a local Vigilance Committee set up in Bombay put pressure on the police to close down the red light district. A crusading Purity Movement journalist called Alfred Dyer had established a newspaper in

Bombay, *The Sentinel*, and in it he fulminated against 'notorious traffickers in European women', 'foreign ruffians', and 'an organised gang . . . the German Jewish Club'.

In England, a respectable number of teenaged girls had actually been abducted to be set to work in brothels abroad, and the unpleasant W. T. Stead, editor of the *Pall Mall Gazette*, proved by going undercover that it was possible to purchase a thirteen-year-old girl in London and spirit her away to Paris. This stunt earned him a three-month prison sentence, but he remained a hero of the Purity Movement. Stead was probably more than a little insane but his activities did play some part in getting the age of consent raised to sixteen.

In the 1890s there was a decline in prostitution in Bombay and the European parts of other major towns as a result of missionary and Purity pressure. The Bombay Midnight Mission patrolled the red light district and tried to dissuade would-be clients. This sometimes led to fisticuffs, and their interference got them into trouble. On occasion the police had to intercede for perfectly innocent women who had been the victims of Purity witch-hunts.

Official dislike of white prostitutes was based on the usual grounds that they threatened the prestige of the ruling nation. Even employment of white barmaids was frowned upon, and Lord Curzon tried to prohibit their employment – but the result of that experiment was that the girls simply doubled their incomes by becoming whores.

LEFT
21 As a trumpeter in the Royal Artillary in the 1930s, Harry Bowen recalls that Kanpur was 'a terrific station'.

BELOW
22 Regardless of public disapproval, visits to brothels were a common feature of military life.

23 W. T. Stead, campaigning journalist for the purity movement. He was obsessed with sex and a female contemporary said that his body 'seemed to exude semen'.

ABOVE RIGHT
24 Josephine Butler, the author and reformer who was a leading member of the purity movement and instrumental in bringing about the repeal of the Contagious Diseases Acts. As a result of her well-meaning but mischievous interference, VD in the British army became difficult to control.

RIGHT
25 The military authorities did try to draw attention to the dangers of VD, but with little success.

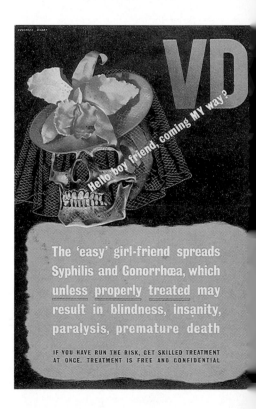

VD

Hello boy friend, coming MY way?

The 'easy' girl-friend spreads Syphilis and Gonorrhœa, which unless properly treated may result in blindness, insanity, paralysis, premature death

IF YOU HAVE RUN THE RISK, GET SKILLED TREATMENT AT ONCE. TREATMENT IS FREE AND CONFIDENTIAL

Regulation Brothels
❧§❧

In Africa, not only was the sale of sex a good way to make money without needing any capital to get started but it also provided a magnificent way for black women to emancipate themselves and improve their status and conditions. This of course ran absolutely counter to the 'moral' tales perpetrated by the Purity campaigners in England about Fates Worse Than Death, and Tickets to Ruin and Poverty, though of course they had the advantage of the limelight. Prostitutes could earn far more than clerks or manual labourers. In Dar es Salaam as late as the 1940s, some of the most affluent and educated citizens were whores. Prostitution there was well organized by the statuesque and beautiful women of the Haya tribe.

In India the authorities had acknowledged that accommodation had to be made for the natural urges of the common soldier: relieved in this manner, there would be less tension and fewer fights in barracks, and there would be fewer violations of local women, which tended to lead to strain between rulers and ruled. On the other hand, contact with prostitutes carried the risk of venereal disease. There were many other far more threatening diseases: cholera, malaria, yellow fever, typhoid, *beriberi* – the list is long; but obvious measures could be taken to avoid VD. Regulated brothels were the answer, and the most widespread form of them was the *lal bazar*.

The *lal bazar* – *lal* means 'red' in Hindi – was a section of the local Indian town in which brothels for the use of servicemen were situated. Usually the brothels were run by an elderly madam who was responsible for cleanliness. The 'Old Bawd' system provided for an average wage of five rupees (paid out of the regimental canteen fund) per madam per month. Neglect of payment could have disastrous results. The Bawd engaged by the 11th Light Dragoons at Mirat abandoned her duties when her payment fell into arrears with the consequence that VD cases in the regiment went from four to twenty-two within three months.

It was however generally difficult to regulate the brothels. Local police peons were organized into small squads to pick up women suspected of having VD, and paid a bounty of between two annas and one rupee, but they were bribable by the girls, who wanted to go on working. It was impossible to control 'vagrant' women, or to prevent their settling near European cantonments. Nor were young soldiers always sensible. They would frequently go to unregistered girls because they were cheaper, on the grounds that they would never themselves catch VD – it would always be the next man.

'Lock hospitals' and VD Laws

∗§ً ∂◊

Another method of control was available to the authorities. As early as the turn of the nineteenth century, concern over VD had led to the establishment of so-called 'lock hospitals' – where diseased girls were literally locked up until cured. These hospitals were not always successful. This was some time before modern cures had been identified, and the long dormancy of some forms of VD – syphilis, for example – was not understood. Girls released from the hospitals might not have been cured. But at any rate they could be kept under strict supervision while they were taking the cure, and the combination of the lock hospital and the *lal bazar* did go quite some way to restrict the spread of venereal disease.

The medical inspection and regulation of brothels system was formalized in Britain in 1866 under the Contagious Diseases Acts, which were introduced in a rather more stringent form in India two years later. These Acts, however, created their own problems. In India, where greater power was given to the police authority in enforcing the Acts, the argument arose that they could be used as an engine for bribery and tyranny against innocent women. Both in England and India the Acts were seen as a licence to violate women, and a powerful campaign was launched against them by the social reformer, Josephine Butler, under the aegis of the Purity Campaign. Religious opponents of the Acts argued that they appeared to condone sin by making it safe. To the forefront in this camp were such men as the Purity Movement journalist Alfred Dyer.

Under sustained pressure over years, the Contagious Diseases Acts were eventually repealed, in England in 1886 and in India two years later. However, the problem of controlling both sexual urge and venereal disease remained. To help solve it, the Military Cantonments Act of 1889 was promulgated, containing a useful clause providing for 'the prevention of the spread of infectious or contagious diseases within a cantonment, and the appointment and regulation of hospitals ... for the reception and treatment of persons suffering from any disease.'

VD had increased dramatically after the closure of the lock hospitals, so now army commanders had a useful weapon to use in the fight to reduce it again. But not for long. The Liberal Government at home was under pressure from the powerful and vocal Purity Movement, who had already smelt a rat, and between 1891 and 1892 two American members of the World's Women's Christian

Temperance Union, Mrs Elizabeth Wheeler Andrew and Dr Kate Bushnell, conducted an investigation funded by Nonconformist money which established that the Cantonments Act was effectively the Contagious Diseases Acts under a new guise. In 1886, Alfred Dyer in *The Sentinel* had published a document which had come into his hand 'emanating from the officer commanding the 2nd Cheshire Regiment, headed "Requisition for extra attractive women for Regimental Bazaar (Soldiers)" . . . . It was addressed to the Cantonment Magistrate, Ambala, who was informed that the regimental strength was 400, that they had six women and needed six more.' Dyer's moral indignation knew no bounds.

Regimental commanders prevaricated in order to protect the practical measures taken to continue to make regulated prostitutes available to their men and so make sex as hygienic as possible – in the mean time the old lock hospitals had been rechristened 'voluntary venereal hospitals'. Brothels were no longer segregated – offically – but in practice they still were by dint of charging more than Indians could afford in those reserved for European use.

All this was in contradiction of British governmental decrees attendant on the repeal of the Contagious Diseases Acts, and the military commanders in India were on a losing wicket. Deregulation of prostitution was insisted upon despite all warnings that this would lead to an increase not only in VD, but also rape, and the soliciting of ordinary local women. The fact that the French and German armies operated regulated brothels with the result that VD was minimalized cut no ice.

By the end of 1896 Army statistics show the number of VD admissions among British troops in India was no fewer than 522 per

1000. This compared with 27 per 1000 in the Germany Army and 44 per 1000 in the French. Public opinion wavered. It was swung when pictures were published of young soldiers dying of tertiary syphilis in the Military Hospital at Netley.

The law was changed again, and the 'reformers' put into retreat. A few years later, in 1910, Paul Ehrlich announced the discovery of an arsenical compound effective in the treatment of syphilis. A corner had been turned.

The machinery of prostitution rolled on regardless. Seaman Donal McKenna had an imagination filled with images of 'dusky maidens'. He was not to be disappointed:

> Japan at that time was very good – that was in 1952. It was good from a seaman's point of view, and it was certainly good from a sexual point of view. Whenever you docked in a Japanese port a customs officer would come aboard and hand out maps of the town. Marked out in a salmon colour on the maps were the districts where the girl houses were. At the time we were getting 1000 yen to the pound, and a girl house would cost about 500 yen. So it was quite exciting.
>
> They were very experienced young ladies, and they were nice girls, not like the Dublin dockside whores. They knew exactly what to do, and they took the initiative, because, of course, as far as they were concerned, it was the old adage of 'Shoot your dust, sailor, time means money.' And that's what they wanted. They wanted you to climax and be away and the next customer in.

> ❧ Contact with prostitutes always meant the risk of vD. In the armed forces it was by now regarded as a self-inflicted disease, and punishment would follow cure. This had the disadvantage of some soldiers' not owning up to having it and therefore making themselves very ill indeed. As for the Merchant Navy, Seaman Donal McKenna recalls the 1950s: 'The Second Officer always used to go round with a medical book, and it had a big plate in the middle of it showing a penis eaten away with vD. It was meant as a warning but nobody paid a blind bit of notice. There was the old joke: Confucius he say: "No such thing as vD. All Tommy rot."'

In Bombay, McKenna found prostitution well organized – 'a good prostitute who worked the ships would have a *Journal of Commerce* in her handbag, so she knew what ship was due to arrive, and when. And then they'd greet you, "You like me, Johnny? I very good for you, Johnny." It was always Johnny. Everybody was Johnny.'

He was under no illusion about brothels: there was nothing elegant about them. In Port Said 'there was a woman who used to come aboard ships, and she was known as Blanket Mary. Of course there were probably plenty of Blanket Marys. They were the girls who'd service the aft crew – the Indian crew.' There was plenty of opportunity ashore for the white crew members, as well as sex shows – 'Watch white man fuck blue-arsed monkey' is one tout's cry he remembers. In Basra there was the Bull Ring: 'Without any shadow of a doubt it was one large brothel. All the girls who were there were business girls, from every age group. Big ones, fat ones, little ones – young boys too. It was pretty crude.' It was patronized by members of the Basra European Club.

Victorian prudishness hung on well into the twentieth century, and the Army had to fight similar battles with public opinion at home as it had done in the nineteenth. When John Sarkies was a Medical Officer in Java, his General sent for him and asked if they could not institute authorized brothels where he could ensure that all the girls were examined, and those who were diseased not be allowed to work: 'I thought that was rather a hot potato to hold for anybody, the question of authorized brothels for the Army was so frowned upon by politicians and MPs who were trying to keep their own voters quiet, of course, and the English are rather prudish I think. The General said, "I see what you mean . . . ."'

A soldier who contracted VD in the 1930s got no pay until he was back on duty. Later, in Madras, John Sarkies was able to keep an informal check on the brothels. He would have a drink with the madam and ask her what precautions she took for her girls. Usually they were inspected by a doctor of the Indian Medical Department, who derived part of his income from this work. It was in the madam's interest to keep her girls clean – but the brothels were not within military jurisdiction by this time: 'I think the madam felt rather satisfied that Senior Medical Officers were taking an interest in the matter. I mean, I had no power to do anything about it, that would have been entirely a civilian matter. The only thing we could do was try to keep the troops under control.'

Dr Ratnabali Chatterjee says that most prostitutes – from the early days on – were recruited from the villages: 'Old prostitutes went out into the villages and procured women by buying them from their fathers, or brothers, or even from their husbands. The criteria were good looks, a good physique, and sometimes virginity'. In Victorian times, once they were in the *lal bazar*, they were certified as prostitutes. If a girl became diseased and was sent to a lock hospital, the process of examination and cure could be painful (a vaginal speculum was used, not always sensitively, by a male doctor), frightening and humiliating. These girls were recruited to serve the British soldiers who had no time or cultural preparation for the niceties and subtleties of India's true professional ladies of pleasure – 'erudite women who were taught not only singing and dancing, but to read and write – some of them were poets themselves.' Their job originally was to initiate young men into correct social and sexual behaviour.

Sex and Punishment

ᥱᢒᢒᥱᥱ

Clearly that was not what the average soldier wanted, coming as he might have done from such a rigorous posting as Razmak on the North-West Frontier. Colonel Wallace Pryke remembers that base as being exclusively male: 'There were no families up there, no females, ladies or anybody . . . even your pet dog couldn't be a bitch . . . .'

Return from such a base, however invigorating the time there might have been in other respects, to the plains station brought a longing for some kind of mixed social life. As far as the men were concerned, 'there could be no arrangements made for a social life except in the NAAFI and in the sergeants' and corporals' messes,' says Pryke.

> They were in the same position really as officers except that there were difficulties if they went to a dance in the town nearest the cantonment. Of course there would be ladies of the night tempting them in these towns and although they were briefed heavily about the dangers of prostitution, inevitably after a few drinks some of them gave way, and there was a system whereby they could clock in before they went out in what was called an Early Treatment Room, and if they signed in again afterwards, having done all the correct things, they would mostly escape punishment if they happened to contract the disease. If they hadn't signed out and signed in again and shown that they'd had treatment then of course they were punished fairly heavily.
>
> Punishment might include having to get into combat dress and double round the barracks square carrying a weighted pack in full view of their fellow soldiers in response to a bugle call which might be sounded several times a day .... Those regiments that developed a bad record were sent to a punishment station – somewhere remote, or unpleasantly hot.

But punishment was not often effective, nor could it curb sexual appetite. Harry Bowen, a Royal Artillery trumpeter in the 1930s, remembers that Kanpur was a 'terrific station. They manufactured a lot of cotton stuffs out there, and for that reason there were a lot of white people there. They'd got a huge social club, and a lot of sporting activities. The military population was very small by comparison.' The barracks were three miles outside the town.

The soldiers employed a large number of Indians as servants. Each soldier had a personal servant or 'boy', who would look after maybe six or seven of them, and get a rupee or two a week from each. In general, relations with the Indians were marvellous. 'They were almost one of us. There were the boys looking after the bunga-lows, and the *syces* looking after the horses, and the women who cleaned the stables, and the *ayahs* who looked after the children in the married quarters.'

Games like football couldn't start until after 5.30 p.m. when the day had cooled down sufficiently, and the main meal was taken later. The evenings might be spent playing lotto, and there were also dances and whist drives. At them, the soldiers might meet beautiful but reserved Parsee women, though dating them there-after didn't happen – except for the occasional lucky officer. As Bowen reflects: 'A soldier's always been looked upon as something not quite up to the standard of the civilians. Because there was always someone who would spoil the evening, there was always the bad egg in the box somewhere that would give them a bad name.'

Anglo-Indian girls seemed to keep themselves to themselves in Kanpur, so that once again any normal, relaxed social mixing with the opposite sex was constricted but the soldiers were catered for in other ways. Bowen remembers:

> There used to be dirty little boys who used to come into the lines and they used to do a sucking motion with their mouth. It might happen that there would be a card school with four play-ing and four more watching, and somebody would come in and whisper to one of the fellows playing cards that there was something going on outside, and he would immediately know

what it was, and he would ask somebody to take his hand at the
card table and go out sharpish and come in about a quarter of
an hour later with a smile on his face and carry on playing
cards. So he'd been satisfied, you see. And this is what had
taken the place of the authorized brothels.

Sex and Segregation
❧

The inability to resolve the question of how to respond to venereal disease meant it was never eradicated. It became a huge
problem to civil as well as military authorities as the British spread their
Empire. In Africa the irony was that whites who wanted protection
from the disease felt threatened by locals who had been infected as a
result of sexual encounters with the colonists themselves. Ray
Roberts, a professor of history at Zimbabwe University, notes that
black female servants were considered a risk to young European
boys, just as local men were seen as a threat to the white women:

> If they were shown any kindness in the home or any degree of
> intimacy they might interpret it wrongly, and would very
> often take advantage of the absence of a male, or misinterpret
> an active kindness or a touch or a look, and resort to rape,
> which in their culture was not as serious an offence as it was in
> Europe . . . . Therefore I think that the Europeans quite rightly
> had some grounds for their fear that they were dealing with a
> dangerous class that was freed from the restraint of its own
> culture and hadn't yet learnt or been taught the necessary
> restraints of Western culture.
>
> In areas where white men were working away from their
> families they would resort to prostitutes, and that very quickly

led to an increase in disease, especially in cities . . . . And a considerable fear did develop that some contact with African men in particular had a certain danger. This is very often exaggerated when women employers would be frightened to have any sort of physical contact, even the touch of their fingers, because they would fear they might catch the disease. The fear was increased by the fact that most domestic servants were men.

Reaction was taken to extremes. On one farm where a servant was suspected of having interfered with a child, the white men of the family castrated him. And the rape laws were tightened up so that, as Roberts says, 'one didn't have to prove rape, attempted rape itself was equally punishable by death. The argument for that stringency was that a white women often, if she'd been raped, would not want to admit such a thing in open court, and therefore the only way in which the criminal could be brought to justice was that she would only have to admit to attempted rape to save her honour, and yet still have the perpetrator punished for what he had done.' This of course meant that many innocent African men were executed for the slightest real or imagined breach of what the white man had decided was sexual propriety.

In the early 1920s, officials in Nairobi wrote of the incurable repugnance for sanitation and hygiene among the local population. Fears of contagion led to calls for segregation within the city, and colonial health official W. J. Simpson, who was responsible for zoning several imperial cities, stressed that separate residential areas were 'absolutely essential for the healthfulness of the locality'.

The shanty town of Pumwani was the result of that segregation. Plots were laid out in 1922 and Africans who were willing were brought from other locations together with their building materials. Those who were unwilling to move had the homes they were living in destroyed.

It was made illegal for African women to reside anywhere else in the city and they could not leave Pumwani after 6 p.m. White men were forbidden to enter the area between sunset and sunrise. Even so, for Pumwani's army of prostitutes it was business as usual with the white man.

Margaret Wiarimu lived and worked there as a prostitute. The girls were divided into different categories. Streetwalkers were known as *watembezi,* and those who solicited outside their houses were *wazi wazi.* Streetwalkers would often specialize in knee-tremblers up against a tree. Few white men ever came down to Pumwani – they would send their houseboys to fetch a girl for them.

Margaret thinks that the white men – most of whom were married, went with her for relaxation. The local men didn't object, as prostitution meant income. Occasionally the girls would be rounded up by the police, but a bribe from a white boyfriend would unlock the cells for them.

Pumwani was created because the British failed to face the facts about prostitution and disease. Instead they just kept on trying to suppress the one and ignore the other. The situation in Pumwani is still the same today, but now poverty and prostitution provide the breeding ground for an even deadlier disease than gonorrhoea or syphilis: AIDS.

5

❧

Missionary Positions

Conversion to Christianity held the occasional benefit for the local pagan – but it was usually of a material rather than a spiritual nature. To some extent Indian women who converted became able to view themselves as less subservient and submissive to their men than they had been; the education which came as a by-product of Christian proselytizing made some Africans literate and enabled them to get better jobs in the towns. Many converted simply as a means to such an end. American missionaries were perhaps a touch freer of the status imperative which burdened their British counterparts. The United States sent men and women black missionaries to South Africa as early as the nineteenth century although slavery was not abolished in North America until 1865 – sixty years after it had been in Britain. (The emancipation of slaves in all British colonies was not, however, achieved until 1834.) Some missionary societies made an effort to identify with the local people. The Salvation Army in India, for example, instructed its members to adopt Indian dress, lifestyle and even names; frequently they also took an Indian spouse. 'Africa was open to missionaries,' recalls Kit Mullan who has lived in both Africa and India. 'They didn't have the same restrictions that we had in India, where you had to respect Hindu and Moslem society. In Africa they had free rein.'

The Shadow of the Cross
≈§≥

Attitudes, however, remained firmly Western Christian wherever missionaries worked. Good intentions could be disastrously misplaced: 'The missionary women,' says historian Ratnabali Chatterjee, 'particularly the reformers, who were very sympathetic, were unable to realize how a woman would want to leave home with a man and become a prostitute because they could not see that it gave the woman a degree of independent earning and a way out of the *purdah* system.' Nautch dancers became the special target of the missionaries in India, according to former diplomat Pran Nevill: 'For missionaries all the traditional art and culture of India was morally wrong and to be censured.' Perhaps one should be grateful that the ancient temples of Khajuraho, with their erotic carvings, remained hidden and protected in the jungle until relatively late in the nineteenth century.

Perhaps one should not judge too harshly: the science of anthropology was far from developed, and missionaries often raised standards of health, nutrition and schooling wherever they were based. However, the price paid by the African, Indian, Solomon Islander, or any other pagan member of the Empire was the surrender of his own culture. Often such cultures proved to be alarmingly fragile when confronted with aggressive north-west European values.

Explorers and developers also saw themselves as infallible standard-bearers for the Christian god. They slaughtered and stole secure in the knowledge that they were doing right; conversion might be a summary business in any case, with no thought given to how much the recipient understood or welcomed the new religion – 'sling a crucifix round their necks and give 'em a handful of beads for their land' was not an unusual sentiment, though it is an extreme example of the thinking, and few colonists would have expressed themselves as baldly as that.

One of the most fundamental sticking-points between native customs and those which the colonizers wished to impose rested on the question of whether or not a man should have more than one wife (or vice versa). Even Sir Richard Burton failed to grasp the nature of polygyny and polyandry as they existed innative cultures: 'Man is by nature polygamic whereas woman as a rule is monogamic,

> ❧ The British Victorians in particular were imbued with a ponderous sense of duty. This, coupled with their unquestioning and habit-bred faith in God and Destiny, together with a conveniently simple and conscience-soothing interpretation of the Darwinian idea of the survival of the fittest, equipped them to go anywhere and do anything and still sleep easily.

and polyandrous only when tired of her lover. For the man, as has been truly said, loves the woman, but the love of the woman is for the love of the man.' The idea of 'love' alone had little place in the social systems the missionaries sought to influence, which were more concerned with marriage as a tool of economics and insurance. The concept of romantic or companionate marriage – and the courtship patterns it engenders – is a typically Western European phenomenon.

As for chastity or the lack of it, that was something much more basic which everyone understood, and although the missionaries handed on the virtues of sexual continence which were important to *their* religion, they didn't all practise what they preached. As Ronald Hyam notes in *Empire and Sexuality*:

> . . . In Papua New Guinea, the Anglican mission suffered resignations over women in the later 1890s and early 1900s. Missionaries complained about digger morals, but the diggers retorted that the mission stations were the worst. The Bishop of North Queensland in 1913-17 J. O. Feetham was indiscreetly eloquent in public about delightful Papuan youths, who seemed to him to combine the character of St John with the physique of Apollo.
>
> In Africa, the missionary had fewer temptations to face than in the Pacific Islands, nevertheless, there was a young transgressor missionary bishop of the Orange Free State, Edward Twells, who fled back to Britain in 1870 to escape a sodomy charge and never held any benefice again before his death thirty years later. And there was a number of eccentrics who aroused a good deal of suspicion and occasionally disgust. Skertchly reported in 1874 that the house of the Wesleyan

146

mission in Dahomey under the Rev. Peter Bernasko had for twenty years been the most notorious brothel on the coast, especially since Bernasko had had sole charge of it since 1863. Bernasko traded in palm oil, got very drunk, neglected his mission, fathered a dozen children, and prostituted his elder daughters. Shortly after arriving in Kenya in 1902 to join the King's African Rifles, [Colonel R.] Meinertzhagen discovered three Italian White Fathers with the Kikuyu at Tusu, doing 'a roaring trade in enticing boys and girls to the mission', there to live a most immoral life: 'they are certainly not "white", but doubtless soon will be fathers.' With them was an Englishman called Smith, who had slept with at least seven girls, saying they could not be true Christians until they had slept with a Christian.

On the other hand, as Merfyn Temple, a missionary in Northern Rhodesia in the 1940s and 1950s and latterly a passionate supporter of African nationalism, recalls, 'There were some missions which simply would not permit any of their Christians to participate in any kind of dancing. Whether they did it quietly or not I don't know, but it was all part of the attack on the sexual *mores* of the people. Because the dancing was a way in which they could express their feeling and their understanding, it was very often a prelude to sexual intercourse.' But there were things which the liberal Temple himself found hard to take at the time: 'The most deplorable thing for me, as a Methodist, was to find the amount of drunkenness there was . . . . I didn't realize of course that beer drinking was very much a part of their culture . . . . They would go on drinking and dancing far into the night. And I'd been taught by the missionaries that really this dancing was a pretty lewd business. And it wasn't really acceptable. One just closed one's eyes to it.'

> ❧ Sexual morality, whether their own or the locals', was a key issue for Imperial Britons, because the British Empire was a Christian empire. From the early days the British abroad considered themselves to be on a divine mission. In the Victorian age missionaries like David Livingstone were superstars, and thousands followed his call to empire for Christianity and commerce. 'I think that the Africans were perfectly correct in thinking that for white people the important thing about morality was sexual morality,' says missionary Merfyn Temple. 'And of course that's why it's been extremely difficult for the Africans to accept Christianity.'

The realities of mission work meant saving souls, and saving souls meant changing people's behaviour. Missionaries became caught up between their concern for people's welfare and their Christian outrage about people's sexual conduct. And Merfyn Temple was aware of many falls from grace amongst the 'educators': 'I was a manager of schools, and there was a number of teachers for whom I was responsible. Sometimes they would have sexual relations with schoolgirls and the local village would report it. In my early days out when my senior missionary had gone and I was on my own, I used to spend an awful lot of time disciplining teachers, and it was always for sexual immorality.'

Buganda: Buggery and Martyrdom
ஃ

Christians weren't the only people seeking converts in Africa. They were preceded in the Kingdom of Buganda by Moslem missionaries. By the 1860s the then ruler, Mutesa, had allowed them to set up a ministry in his country. The Moslems had no objection to certain sexual practices of the Baganda people, but when the Christians arrived in 1877 they were appalled to discover that buggery appeared to be quite usual in the upper echelons of society. What neither Moslem nor Christian outsider realized was that the Buganda leadership was using the religious factionalism they had introduced to play its own political game.

Over a century later, the spot where the Christian missionaries built their first church is occupied by a great cathedral. Its windows commemorate a series of events which took place at the *Kabaka*'s – the king's – court between 1885 and 1887. By that time, Mwanga had succeeded Mutesa. He held absolute sway over his people. He was homosexual, and enjoyed the right to have any of his pageboys. After the arrival of the missionaries, converts among them began to refuse his advances. Fearful that the missionaries were turning his subjects against him, or that his subjects were themselves using Christianity as an excuse to question their obedience to him, Mwanga indulged in a series of killings. IN 1885, three Protestant boys from Alexander Mackay's Church Missionary Society were killed. In June 1886, thirty-one Catholic and Protestant boys and young men were burned on a huge funeral pyre at Namugongo. A further group was slaughtered early in 1887. Interestingly, Mwanga did not extend the killing to the boys' families, nor did he force the missionaries to leave. It must be assumed that he felt that he had made his point; an absolute ruler he may have been; but he still had to have the support of the majority of his court behind him to maintain power.

At the spot where they died, African Catholics built a huge shrine to their first saints – twenty-two of the martyred boys were canonized in 1964. To Catholics, they had suffered death rather than return to the pagan ways of their fathers. Ironically , Mwanga himself converted in the end, but was eventually ousted from power and died in exile in the Seychelles in 1903.

The Unkind Cut?

◆§§◆

Clashes over sexuality continued, and in Kenya in the 1920s and 1930s one custom became the centre of a conflict that threw the missions into turmoil and challenged the very basis of British colonial rule. This time sexuality and Christianity came to a head over the Kikuyu tribe's practice of female circumcision. Helen Dadet, the daughter of an eminent black cleric, and now an educationalist at Jomo Kenyatta University, remembers that the operation 'was done first thing in the morning. The girls would go to the place where the ritual was performed. All the women would gather there . . . . The missionaries interpreted the traditional female circumcision ritual as barbaric. They did not see what it represented to the community. They simply saw it as a cruel rite which had no reason to exist.' They made no attempt to understand it, or they would have found out that no Kikuyu traditionalist would have taken a wife who was uncircumcised. For many years the Kikuyu believed that if a woman had not been through the operation she could not bear children, and they had no evidence to the contrary.

Jane Chege, who has carried out much research into the British administration's attitude towards female circumcision, explains, 'For the Kikuyu people, female circumcision was very, very important, in the sense that through it a person moved from childhood to adulthood. Adulthood was not just a biological state, it was full of religious and social meaning. If a woman who was not circumcised had had a child, the gods and the spirits of the ancestors would have been offended, and the whole community would have been made to suffer.'

The Kikuyu live in the highlands of central Kenya. Here, the Church Missionary Society established a mission at Kahuhia in 1906. Cyril Hooper grew up here, where his grandfather, father and mother came to preach, educate, and help the people. The Hoopers worked hard to develop the mission. They built a church and made a clearing for a football field. All the time they were telling the Kikuyu about the way of the Christian god. For Cyril's grandfather, Douglas Hooper, acceptance of it meant that the Kikuyu had to abandon their traditional customs.

As Cyril Hooper says, 'He certainly thought they were bad, that they were putting people down, and taking people to Satan. My father took a much broader view. He felt that a Christian way of thinking should be brought to bear on existing conditions. The only thing that worried him seriously was the rite of female circumcision – possibly more from the physical point of view, and the way in which it spoilt all the feelings of sex and sex life for the girl, and made her an open doorway for a man to use as he liked.' Jane Chege adds, 'The missionaries felt that it was actually a degradation of the soul, because it was a mutilation of the body, which they saw as the temple of God. And of course they regarded the ceremonies which surrounded both male and female circumcision as heathen.'

In 1922, Cyril Hooper's mother, Elizabeth, founded a boarding-school at Kahuhia for girls from all over the district. As the 1920s wore on, girls' circumcision became an ever-increasing source of concern for parents, teachers and pupils. A letter written at the time by one teacher, Ethel Soles, to Elizabeth Hooper, charts the develop-ing crisis:

> When I went down to Mombasa, five small girls were to stay for the holidays . . . . Miss Wiseman was here [at the school] in charge, and she said that for a few days they were quite happy. Then, when she happened to be off the station for an hour or two, Wambui's mother came and took them off. It was too late for Miss Wiseman to go up [to the village] that evening, but she went with Levi the next day. Duadi himself was there, but all their efforts were useless, and [the girls] were circumcised very soon. You can imagine my feelings when I heard this news, and poor Miss Wiseman is very upset too.

Circumcision was against the school rules, and there was an endless game of cat and mouse as the missionaries tried to prevent the girls from running away or being taken by their parents for circumcision, as another letter, of January 1930, testifies:

> You will be glad to hear that we have an uncircumcised girl of about fifteen years of age in the dormitory. At the beginning of this term our senior girl, Esther Wanjaru, came to ask if she might go to the village not far from her own to rescue a girl

> who, being uncircumcised, was being persecuted. This girl used
> to be in a dormitory at Ngenda, which is connected with
> Kambui Gospel Mission. The dormitory had been closed owing
> to furlough, leaving ten girls to be sent home to their villages,
> all of whom have since given in [to circumcision] with the
> exception of this one, Wanjiku wa Kimani. Well, we were very
> full up, but I felt we must try and take this lass in.

In the mean time, the missionaries were conducting a battle against
polygyny; but, as Cyril Hooper remembers, Ethel Soles 'came to
sleep in the same house as my family, and my father used to have
his leg pulled as he walked back to the house: "So you're going back
to your wives, eh?" the locals would say, and they would laugh
about it . . . . Now, Grandfather had made it a rule that people
sinned when they took more than one wife. They were still allowed
to come to church, but they were not allowed to take communion.'

The rigorous enforcement of Church rules was supported by
another mission group in Kikuyu country. Dr John Arthur was a
medical man who led a team of committed Presbyterians at the
Church of Scotland Mission. They believed that female circumcision
was an evil which had to be eradicated. Arthur was especially im-
patient with the Kikuyu Central Association, a proto-political group
of Kenyans who saw circumcision as vital to Kikuyu identity. The
struggle developed bitterly during the 1920s. In 1929, Arthur travelled around Kikuyu districts campaigning against the circumcision
rite. By then there was a boarding-school for boys at Kahuhia as well,
and Ben Ngumba, a pupil at the time, remembers Dr Arthur's visit:

> He had some people with him – not many, maybe three or
> four. And we were called to the church to attend a meeting he

was holding. There were no women present. There were our teachers, us boys, and some local businessmen and politicians. Dr Arthur gave us a very interesting lecture on women's circumcision. He explained the dangers of circumcising women, and showed that the operation not only put the women in danger but could make it difficult for them to bear children.

There was an uproar. Anyone who seemed to agree with Dr Arthur was booed, and insults flew. The meeting broke up.

Ben Ngumba's family was not in favour of female circumcision, but that did not prevent one of his own younger sisters being taken away and submitted to the ritual.

Kikuyu feelings were aroused – the Kikuyu Central Association saw the issue as a useful peg to hang its political ambitions on, and the debate snowballed. Counter-arguments to the medical ones put forward by Arthur were produced. Even today, Atta Wambui, an elderly Kikuyu woman, vehemently disagrees with Arthur. She was circumcised, and had fourteen children, seven boys and seven girls. She still believes that the ability to give birth without problems depends upon the shape of the pelvic bone, and that Arthur was either scaremongering, or attempting to denigrate Kikuyu customs. or both. One wonders if Arthur was able to explain that scar tissue does not stretch. Clearly if he was, he didn't convince.

Jane Chege also feels that the missionaries exaggerated the dangers: 'Because you find that most of the people that you talk to – the older women who practised circumcision, and even those who practise it up to this day – you find that they are not adversely affected. It's hard to find Arthur's arguments convincing, in the sense that these women give birth to many children, and in pre-colonial society, the same thing happened.'

The Church of Scotland Mission remained on the offensive. Its missionaries decided that their church members should be made to sign a declaration renouncing circumcision. News of this spread quickly. 'People became very angry,' says Ben Ngumba, 'particularly the ones who were politicians and they started talking about it, and a dance was started, and this dance had very bitter words against missionaries, settlers and colonialists . . . . The dance used to take place in darkness because nobody was allowed to dance in the open, and if they were known to have danced or if they were caught dancing they would have been arrested and imprisoned.'

The Kikuyu believed that white men would not have sex with circumcised girls. If girls remained uncircumcised, the white men would take them. These fears found expression in lewd songs. As Ben Ngumba recalls, 'They used to say that the white men were trying to create prostitutes among the Kikuyu and that later on these girls would become the wives of settlers and other colonialists who might come.'

On 31 October 1929, after a month's grace, the African elders of the Church of Scotland Mission were summoned together to sign the declaration, but after a morning of prayer, one by one they refused. 'I shall remain a Kikuyu; I will continue to circumcise,' they said.

One of Ethel Soles' letters reflects the mood and the tension of the time:

> . . . At Kahuhia and Kambui they are having the most serious trouble. The [Kikuyu Central] Association are demanding girls' circumcision and Dr Arthur has made a drastic rule, more

> especially for his teachers and agents ... this has caused an awful upheaval, teachers have left and in some of the schools there are very few attending at all – girls have run away from their dormitories for circumcision .... I have never seen Dr Arthur so depressed. He said at the prayer meeting on Tuesday that their whole work was shaken to the foundations.

Atta Wambui adds, 'The missionaries wrote so many letters to those parents who had brought their children here for education. They all came over and they tore the letters into pieces. There was an uproar. One Kikuyu man who was their representative went up to the front and said, "Now that these people have brought in this rule, we are going to take our girls away and we are going to continue circumcising. We will not go by this law."' After her own circumcision, Atta Wambui stopped going to school completely. She and her friends were banished from the Church for three years.

For the nationalist politicians the crisis was a windfall. Jane Chege remembers that 'the controversy actually gave a weapon to the Kikuyus who were agitating for self-government because they could use it as a rallying-cry for support on another, actually much more important issue, which was that of land. The settlers had taken away their land and they wanted it back. They also wanted to keep their culture and to be self-governing.' Missionaries were seen as the accomplices of the settlers: the latter took the land, the former took the beliefs of the locals. In Northern Rhodesia missionary Merfyn Temple was once on the receiving end of the nationalist reaction:

> There was an occasion when I was having tea with my wife, outside the Mission House, on a Sunday afternoon, under the big fig tree; and out of the bush emerged an African. The

African people on mission station would leave us quietly on a Sunday so I was surprised to see anybody coming; normally nobody would dream of disturbing me. He was dressed in rather ragged clothes, tatty shorts, and he simply came over and handed me a letter. It was written in good English on a sheet of exercise book paper: 'I want to tell you that you are the one who has come here to apply Bible grease. And when the time of the revolution comes, you will be one of the first people to be hanging from the fig tree.' So I thanked him and he went away. I asked someone later if they could explain to me what Bible grease was. He replied, 'Well, what people are saying in the village is that you missionaries have come to work with the colonial government in order to keep us soft. That's the grease. You see, they use the grease to soften the hides, and they think it will keep the people soft enough to go on accepting colonial rule.' I also learned later that they thought the missionaries were introducing more white people into the area so that they could come and make their farms there, and take the Africans' land.

In Kenya the tension erupted into real violence. On the night of 1 January 1930 a seventy-year-old American missionary, Hulda Stumpf, irascible but holding no special brief for Dr Arthur's views, was preparing for bed when an intruder broke in. Her body was found the following morning. She had been circumcised, and, it was alleged, raped. In fact later investigation showed no evidence of rape, or even attempted rape, though the government deemed it politically expedient to put this out as the crime committed, rather than circumcision. She was already partially undressed at the time her attacker entered through the window, and she undoubtedly suffered a brutal death. The pillow used to suffocate her – before the operation on her clitoris and labia was performed – was pressed down with sufficient force to break her nose. Nothing was stolen, and there was no vandalism.

Both Dr Arthur and the Governor of Kenya, Sir Edward Grigg, used the murder to further their campaign against circumcision. Arthur, a stubborn man with an inflated idea of his own importance, wrote to the Church of Scotland Mission's patroness, Lady Atholl, to enlist her support. Following the incident, the British exerted greater pressure on the Kikuyu activists. A get-tough policy proscribed public meetings as well as the notorious protest dancing with its scurrilous songs. But the general reaction of the missionaries to her death was one of shock tinged with guilt.

The rift neither healed nor did the issue go away. Instead, independent Churches were founded by black Kenyan Christians which respected local customs, and these churches – the African Independent Pentecostal Church and the African Orthodox Church – were the real cradle of the Kenyan nationalist movement. They founded their own schools. 'In them,' remembers educationalist Helen Dadet, 'people were taught that they were Africans and that they must hang on to their identity, because it was proper and not wrong to belong to a given community.'

But by the time of the Mau Mau rebellion in the mid-1950s, circumcision had come under discussion once again. 'There was a resurgence of nationalism then,' says Helen Dadet. 'People revived their sense of cultural identity, and female circumcision was part of it.' She was at school at Kahuhia at the time:

> Actually at one point I thought it might have been a good thing, because all my friends in the village got circumcised, and to me they looked like they were proper grown-ups. They

behaved differently, because just before the ritual and while they were recuperating after it the girls are given a lot of cultural, social, and feminine education. And I kind of envied what I saw in them, and I said to myself, surely, if circumcision makes people change like that it must be a good thing.

But my own parents never talked to me about it. All I do remember was that they would keep me from going to watch when the ritual was on.

Her own father had had major rows with his father over his rejection of the Kikuyu religion in favour of Christianity. Her grandfather had been a medicine man, and was heartbroken when he realized that his son was not going to continue the tradition. 'I could rightfully say that people of my father's generation were the first who actually made a personal decision of commitment to Christianity and abandoning the traditional religion. And to be able to make such a decision, one had to be quite brave.'

The issue smouldered on; but what was perhaps most important was not whether female circumcision was a good or bad thing, morally or physiologically, *per se*, but whether foreign settlers, however much more advanced they considered themselves to be, and however much they felt they were interfering for the good of the locals, had any *right* to interfere. Merfyn Temple says, 'I gave no credit for the fact that we had tried to invade a society and a culture which for hundreds of years had developed their own very satisfactory ways of organizing their lives. I simply assumed that my way was the right way and theirs was wrong.' Helen Dadet says, 'By saying that you don't want girls to be circumcised, you are getting too close to what holds society together. You are getting too close to what makes a Kikuyu woman feel that she's a full woman. You are touching on people's sense of value, sense of identity, sense of well-being. And if you play with what makes somebody feel like somebody, you are inviting a crisis . . . . You must leave somebody something that they can call their own.'

26 Ethel Soles, headmistress, surrounded by demurely uniformed pupils of the Kahuhia Secondary School for Girls, Kenya.

BELOW LEFT 27 Successive generations of missionaries were not unusual. Here, Cyril Hooper and his father (centre) are celebrating the Golden Jubilee of the mission at Kahuhia. The mission was founded in 1906 by Cyril Hooper's grandfather.

RIGHT 28 Hulda Stumpf, the American missionary murdered and circumcised in January 1930 in the wake of an attempt by the Church of Scotland Mission forcibly to put an end to the practice of ritual female circumcision among the Kikuyu people.

29 Patson Travers (second from left) with friends at a party in Salisbury, Rhodesia, in the 1960s. Patson, the son of a white father and a black mother, found work as a government chauffeur, but during his schooldays and subsequently he frequently found himself rejected by both black and white society.

BELOW 30 Afro-Asian conflict: Maria Brennan (right) with her sisters Fatima and Amina and her brother Abdul at St John's Convent School for Coloured Children in Salisbury, Rhodesia in 1947. Maria, born Halima Osman, converted to Christianity there, outraging her strict Moslem family.

6

❦

Children of Empire

Oh East is East, and West is West, and never
  the twain shall meet,
Till Earth and Sky stand presently at God's
  great Judgement Seat;
But there is neither East nor West, Border,
  nor Breed, nor Birth,
When two strong men come face to face,
  though they come from the
  the ends of earth!

The Ballad of East and West
Rudyard Kipling (1865–1936)

The British Empire was the forum for the largest encounter between different peoples the world has ever seen. It was not an absolute melting-pot, but the combination of local race and European reached a high number of permutations: there were creoles and mulattos, for example; Euro-Africans, Anglo-Indians, quadroons and octoroons. The importation of Indians to Africa to work on the railways and do clerical and routine administrative work led to the mixed race of Afro-Asians.

No Man's Land
⊷⊱⊱

The British called the children who resulted from the couplings of black and white people, 'coloured'. From the end of the eighteenth century in India, and virtually from the first in Africa, these people, always a minority of course, led a half-life, belonging neither to the European nor the local camp, and mistrusted by both sides. From the point of view of the pure-bred local, the 'half-caste' was not dependable because he might very well, when it came to the crunch, side with the white man; to the colonizer, the 'coloured' was a reminder that plenty of empire-builders breached one of the fundamental taboos and had sex with the natives. 'Half-castes' came in a variety of shades of colour; some were virtually indistinguishable from whites. According to Iris MacFarlane, a teenager in India in the 1930s, there were small physical signs by which you could identify them, and, as has been hinted too, they were distinguishable by the kind of work they did. Because the whites believed that in a crisis the 'half-caste' population would side with them, they gave them jobs in key areas: they would be the people employed in the railway and in the ports; in radio and telegraph offices, and as firemen, nurses, skilled workers and drivers. Many converted to Christianity – in the eighteenth century a bounty was offered to those who would; and there was also the incentive of self-improvement that conversion afforded. But they were never wholly taken into anyone's confidence.

The unhappiness started early in life. Patson Travers grew up when Zimbabwe was still Rhodesia and under white rule: 'My parents were not married. I was the result of what we popularly call a

162

hit and run accident and I grew up with my mother, in all perspectives in the African community.' There were few schools available to 'coloureds' in those strictly segregated days and Travers didn't start his education until he was eleven years old.

> I had an uncle who worked in what we now call Cherugwyn. He wrote to the Native Commissioner in Kwe-Kwe and told him that there was a coloured child in the African location who was not going to school, and he requested assistance for me. The result of that was that we were literally arrested by the Native Commissioner. The *askaris* came to our home and we went before the Native Commissioner, who asked why I was not at school, and my mother, being illiterate, said unfortunately, 'I don't know – what school can I put him to? You know, he's not black, he's not white, he's in-between.' And the Native Commissioner told her, 'Enrol him at any school that will admit him.' So I was enrolled in an African school at Kwe-Kwe.
>
> I lasted three days because among the children at that school I stuck out like a sore thumb and they called me *morungu*, which in Shona means 'a white man'; and I was bullied so much in those three days that I decided that I was not going back to school. I didn't tell my mother this. I just went AWOL and went back home when I was expected, like at lunch-time.
>
> When eventually my mother found out that I had left the school, she enrolled me at a coloured school, and at the coloured school there was another reason why I was not accepted: I looked like them all right but unfortunately I couldn't speak a word of English, and they also knew that I lived in the African location, so the kids gave me hell. And they called me a *kaffir* and a *munt*.

Most children of mixed blood had similar experiences.

Prejudice and Harassment
◦§◦

Eurasians – as they were called in India until the mid-twentieth century (Anglo-Indian until that time was the name given to the British resident in India) – under British rule were less privileged than under other colonizers. The Dutch, for example, were especially tolerant even of inter-marriage. During the seventeenth century affairs and marriages between Indians and English were perfectly acceptable, and as we have seen, Eurasians were employed by the East India Company. Governor-General Cornwallis' move to get rid of them in the late eighteenth century came as work for the Company became more attractive and better paid. The Eurasians were squeezed out by whites who were after their jobs, and from 1791 they were excluded from joining the civil, military and marine services of the Company. The official reason given out for this was that the Indians despised them, and that the locals needed to have nothing but respect for those in authority. There was a grain of truth in this: but pious Hindus regarded *all* Europeans as unclean, whether of pure or mixed blood, and in practice Indians did not resent Eurasian administrators. In the Company armies, Eurasian officers like James Skinner commanded the respect and affection of their troops.

The rechartering of the Company in 1833 forbade the practice of prejudice in making appointments, but it was a long time before equal rights were restored to Anglo-Indians. 'Gentlemanliness' was deemed a quality desirable in the selection process, and was used to weed out Anglo-Indians who had otherwise been successful in the examinations which had been introduced for applicants to Company posts: mere patronage was no longer enough. Sometimes, the examination results were rigged; but this was a rearguard action on the part of conservative elements within the Company's administration.

Notwithstanding their treatment, the Anglo-Indian population supported the British at the time of the Indian Mutiny. The reforming Indian Civil Servant C. E. Trevelyan, one of the Anglo-Indians' English champions, bemoaned their fate, caught as they were permanently between two cultures and races, and belonging properly to neither. He made sure they got fair treatment in competition for work during his governorship of Madras from 1859 onwards. Anglo-Indians made very good doctors, and were happily accepted by their white female patients – though white men were less pleased at such arrangements. When an Anglo-Indian called Josiah Dashwood Gillies, MD, MRCS (St Andrew's), returned to Madras shortly before Trevelyan's appointment and unwisely chose to specialize in gynaecology, he found himself in serious trouble after the death of one of his patients. The fact that he knew more about medicine than the local white Inspector-General of Hospitals, and did not hesitate to demonstrate this, did not help his case, and though he was exonerated in the end, his career was damaged, as the investigating authority decided that he was wanting in the area of 'gentlemanliness'.

Anglo-Indian missionaries sometimes found themselves at the mercy of the lower-class prejudices of their Nonconformist white colleagues, and even *white* female missionaries ran an especial risk of being exposed to scandal, working as they did with Indian Christians. Englishmen were quick to point the finger at missionary societies which put 'their young ladies at the mercy of lascivious Hindu men.'

In 1870, Mary Pigot took over the Church of Scotland's orphanage and women's mission in Calcutta. She got on well with her white colleagues and with the local Indian Christians, and for nine years worked happily and successfully there. However, in 1879 the able but domineering Reverend William Hastie arrived in Calcutta and started throwing his weight around in Presbyterian circles, soon irritating an Indian colleague of Mary's whom he took to have criticized his views in *The Indian Christian Herald*. He told the man, 'You . . . cannot understand the Free Church controversy, no mere native Christian can.' Then he tried to interfere in the work of the women's mission, and to forbid Mary Pigot from continuing to associate with her colleague. She opposed Hastie, and their relationship deteriorated fast.

Hastie then began a campaign of harassment of Mary Pigot. He accused her – quite wildly – of 'immorality' on the grounds that she had been seen at a picnic organized by the Church sitting on the same reclining chair as Professor Wilson, a senior lay teacher. He also accused her of harbouring Roman Catholic sympathies. Miss Pigot fought back, and took Hastie to court. The presiding judge was Mr Justice Norris, not noted for his liberal opinions on questions of race. Professor Wilson spoke in her defence, as did her Indian colleagues, with whom Hastie had also accused her of intimacy. It was all to little avail, despite the fact that Hastie manifestly had no case. Norris wouldn't trust the Indian's evidence, and was in a rush to get away on holiday – he said as much in court – and the case was dragging on. To be fair, he gave no credence to Hastie and found in favour of Mary Pigot, but he awarded her only one anna in damages, and ordered each party to pay their own costs. In the course of the trial, Mary had been obliged to prove her own legitimacy, and during one two-hour period had had to submit to over 300 questions. But it was clear that Hastie had behaved very shabbily and hypocritically – he had been perfectly willing to allow Mary to continue her work at the mission if she accepted his authority, notwithstanding his 'suspicion' of her immorality. This too was pointed out by Norris in court.

A subscription was got up to allow Mary to appeal, and this she did successfully in the following year, 1884. She was awarded 3000 rupees' damages, and costs – a total of 12 000 rupees. Hastie was relieved of his position. He went home to Scotland to defend himself, omitting to pay Mary's costs. Failing to justify himself to the General Assembly in Edinburgh, after subjecting them to a speech lasting eight hours, he returned to Calcutta where a separate commission of enquiry was under way. Before leaving, as a precaution to safeguard his savings, he made over £300 to his mother and sister. When he arrived in Calcutta he was arrested for failure to pay Mary's damages and costs, but was able to prove his insolvency and thus avoided parting with a penny. Mary, however, was vindicated, and awarded a pension of £40 a year by the Foreign Mission Committee. Hastie went back to Scotland, where ten years later he emerged as Professor of Theology at Glasgow University.

If Mary had not been an Anglo-Indian, the wretched man might not have saved his career quite so spectacularly.

'Orphaned' and Unwanted
⋖§§⋗

But it was the children of the white fathers and local mothers who suffered most. Another Scotsman, John Anderson Graham, was appalled at their plight, and in 1900 established orphanages for them in Kalimpang. The children, as Howard O'Connor, the present Principal of Kalimpang School, remembers, 'were an embarrassment to the British father, who would finally, being a young man probably on his first service in India, go home, find himself a British bride and come back to India not wanting to have anything to do with his former mistress or his children by her. The children were just something that had to be swept under the carpet, and if there was a man like Dr Graham who was willing to take care of the problem, officialdom was perfectly happy to help him.'

Conscience-salving cash came from leading members of the British élite like the Governor of Bengal, and merchant companies like Whiteway and Laidlaw. Graham was able to use the money to provide an education for the children who were brought to him. Marie Godfrey is an Anglo-Indian who came to Kalimpang in 1917:

> My father came from Burma. He was a Britisher and he worked for the Nizam's railways. All that was written on his marriage certificate. That's the only reason I know. He died when he was still in service here [in India]. My mother was a Miss Taylor to start with, then she married my father and we were in Lucknow for a long time. My sister and I were very young when he died. We had an elder brother but he emigrated to England and died there . . . . My mother was not well off and

she couldn't pay for our education. She heard of this Anglican school and applied for us and we were accepted because they were taking Anglicans first. We were about eight years old.

We had a house-mother and a house-aunt. Both ladies were from Britain. They looked after us, but we had to do all our own bedmaking and washing and cleaning .... I must say it was a wonderful school.

Dr Graham wanted to see the children in his care grow up distanced from their Indian roots. All the teachers were European. One of his principles was that the local mother was never allowed to visit her child. As the father didn't want anything to do with them, the children effectively grew up as orphans.

We had no more contact with our mother until we were about thirteen or fourteen years old, when she came up once. And most of the children were like that .... I didn't feel sad, though. We had forgotten all about our mother, you see, because we were so very young when we went to Dr Graham's; and we seldom got a letter. It was very strange when we did see her again because we didn't know her. But she stayed for a fortnight and so we had an opportunity to get to know her a bit. She brought us dolls and all sorts of treats. But we didn't see her again until we left school.

The mothers felt the separation very badly – there were stories of how mothers would go to the compound and hide in the shrubbery just to catch a glimpse of their children. They would long to call out to them and go and touch them, but they didn't dare, for fear of jeopardizing the child's future. Some couldn't withstand the temptation, though, and frequently caused themselves more pain – the child would not recognize his or her mother, there would be embarrassment and emotional distress.

Shame and embarrassment would follow the Anglo-Indian children into the outside world. Like thousands of other Anglo-Indian girls, Marie Godfrey became a nurse. In the course of time she met an Englishman who became her boyfriend, but 'the British had no time for the Anglo-Indians. No time for them .... A Britisher couldn't mix with an Anglo-Indian. He couldn't mix. There was no question of marriage. The same thing happened to my sister. She went to England and met a man, but the war came and that was that .... The man I was friendly with had come to the hospital to visit a sick friend and that is how I met him. He was a very nice man. Never missed church on a Sunday. He was very good.' They met in 1931 and continued to see each other until the outbreak of war, when he joined the Navy and went away. 'I don't want to talk about him. I don't want him to know. The one and only man I *ever* knew.' They had a lot in common, they preferred the outdoor life – walks and excursions – to dances. 'He never worried about what people would think. He was an electrical engineer so he was in a senior position. He did lots of good, for example, he organized crèches for the women workers ....'

She did see her boyfriend again – in Bombay. By then he had become engaged to an admiral's daughter. He wrote to ask her to meet him. 'He told me all about the girl. I said, "Oh, well, I'm glad you're going to be happy." He went back to England and broke off the engagement. He told me that he became very ill afterwards. I heard all about it later.' He returned again to India – to Calcutta, for medical treatment and to recuperate. But he still didn't propose to

Marie, and when he returned to England again he married someone else. Marie saw him again on another trip he made to India after the war. 'He came out with his wife. He had a son. He came to see me once. And I said, "Yes, I know you're married. You wrote and told me about it," and that sort of thing. "But I don't expect you to visit me any more. I would not accept it if I was your wife." So . . . he was very good. He never came back. He never tried to come back and see me. But they didn't stay long. They couldn't stand India – the wife and child – they couldn't stand India so they packed up and went off to England and I've never heard of them since.'

It was all right, of course, to enjoy the society of Anglo-Indian girls, who tended to be more relaxed than the English girls, and whose company was sought by the men left behind in the summer when the memsahibs had departed for Simla and the other hill stations. 'I organized a cricket match, ladies versus gents, to raise money for the war fund,' says District Officer Douglas Stanton-Ife:

> ॐ There were some marriages between soldiers and Anglo-Indians. The husbands were known as 'Bombay Jocks,' remembers Royal Artilleryman Harry Bowen. 'They weren't frowned on, but they weren't fussed over a lot either. They became a separate section of the unit. It was the same if you had an Anglo-Indian man in the unit – he was different from the others. And yet he might be a very nice chap. Some of them were very good hockey players, for a start.'

I may mention that the ladies had to be imported. No local ladies could appear in public playing cricket against gentlemen. They were imported from Guya, which was the district head-quarters, and they were almost all Anglo-Indian.

They were nice and jolly and not in the least intellectual – Anglo-Indians seldom are. But it was a very pleasant occasion for me because I was so lonely, and hardly ever saw an attract-ive woman. It was delightful just to see a lot of girls running about playing cricket.

Rupert Mayne, who went to India to work in a jute mill in the 1930s, also remembers happy evenings spent with Anglo-Indian girls when the memsahibs were up in the hills. There would be impromptu parties 'you'd lay on the drinks, lay on some dancing, lay on a buffet, and rally together some girls. But one did not mix with them in the cold weather. They were just as proper as the white girls, but they were a lot of fun. I don't think they often mar-ried white people.'

But what kind of life did the jolly Anglo-Indian girls go home to?

Anglo-Indian Edna Pierce suffered terribly at the hands of her first husband, who was also Anglo-Indian, though his skin colour was much lighter and he and his family – who were similarly light-skinned – identified strongly with the whites. Only her father-in-law was sympathetic.

When my first daughter was born, they said, 'Is she fair or is she black?' . . . . They were very cruel to me. My sisters-in-law used to take me to dances, and then beat me up. They'd catch me by the hair and twist me round on the dance floor and kick me. Once they had a brooch with a pin and they stuck it into my stomach when I was pregnant. I lost that child. My father took them to court and they came to me begging for forgiveness. Another time my husband hit me so hard in the eye that he blinded me. I stuck to the marriage because of my daughter, and because of the vows. But my father couldn't stand it, and begged me to leave.

In the end her husband deserted her.

The Uncertain Future

In 1947, the British left India for good. The Anglo-Indians remained behind, on both sides of the frontier that now divided a formerly united country into Hindu India and Moslem Pakistan. The Anglo-Indians were an island of Englishness with an uncertain future. 'The Indian community at large found it difficult to accept that although the British had gone, this legacy of the British continued to live on in the country,' comments Howard O'Connor. 'Integration was slow to come about. We still search for Anglo-Indians who should be able to trace their line of descent to a British male ancestor, but the number we find each year is smaller and smaller – either due to emigration, death, or assimilation.'

Across the Indian Ocean in Zimbabwe, the children of black-and-white unions have continued to live in a social no-man's land since the war of independence. Rhodesia – as the country was then called – was a colony in which racial integration was totally rejected. Its white former leader, Ian Smith, recalls:

Integration wasn't an easy problem to deal with because in the main under the old British system we tried to preserve our tra-

ditions, our heritage and our culture. We were white people –
Europeans; but we found ourselves in the early pioneering days
of the colony in a situation where there was obviously a short-
age of white women. I think whenever this has happened in the
world, history shows that where you have a crossing of the
races it was white men with black women, not the reverse.
Now, one of the problems there was that the child of such a
union was a coloured child, but brought up by a black mother
under her traditions and speaking her language; so the difficulty of incorporating such a child into the white community
was obviously compounded.

Against that, 'coloured' Patson Travers remarks: 'It was a question
of divide and rule, and that was the British system. At some stage or
other someone must have woken up to the fact that they could not
remain in Africa forever as masters, and so, to make it more difficult
for any uprising to succeed, they would divide the people into different classes and give them separate favours.'

❧ The position of the 'coloured' population was crucial to the white government of Rhodesia, which, by the time Ian Smith became Prime Minister in 1964, was on the defensive. He says, 'You know, in Africa we lived cheek by jowl with this black nationalism which was emerging, and we had seen what had happened in countries like Ghana and Nigeria, and of course Kenya, nearer home, where the whites had previously been led to believe that there would have been a home for them out there, but subsequently had to leave, and the stories which were passed on to us through these people weren't very encouraging. It all hinged on matters like these. The fact is that when the black man came to power the white man got short shrift, and his possessions were literally confiscated.'

Caught in the middle, mixed race children from all over Rhodesia and its neighbouring colonies ended up at the school of St John's Convent in the capital, Salisbury – now Harare. But segregated education was central to producing the racial hierarchy which the white settlers wanted. Patson Travers says, 'I became convinced that I was different in every sense of the word – I was not white, and I was not black – when I went to St John's, because all the children there were coloured children. St John's was more or less like an orphanage. Although we had some children there whose fees were paid by their parents, and who were taken away every holiday, some of us stayed almost on a permanent basis.'

The teachers were German Dominican nuns. Sister Aurea Wintel started work there in the late 1950s: 'The sisters felt very strongly that they should give the pupils practical skills, in the hope that some of them might fit into society later on and be equipped to do so. We taught sewing, embroidery, carpet-weaving, carpentry and metalwork.' Former students remember the regime as tough. Abdul Osman was there a generation or so earlier: 'They treated us very rough. Every punishment they used a whip, a belt, a donkey-belt or a stick. They were never kind people. They didn't like us . . . . Once we were on a truck going out to pick cotton on the school farm, and I think the driver went over a ridge so that some of the children were thrown out. Those that were thrown clear were lucky, but I fell under the wheels and the truck ran over me – it broke my pelvis in half.'

Until Zimbabwean independence, when segregation in schools was discontinued, St John's qualified generations of mixed race children to hold positions that were superior to the blacks'; and these children were loyal to the colonial regime. Latterly, there was no attempt to convert Hindus or Moslems to Christianity, and Sister Aurea knows of only one Moslem girl pupil – Maria Brennan – who, without her parents' permission, embraced the Catholic faith while at school. Abdul Osman's experience a few years earlier was that pressure was very definitely put on children to convert.

Maria Brennan is Abdul's sister and the granddaughter of a wealthy and powerful Moslem of mixed race, Hadji Osman, whose family contained pure black and coloured elements, and so was subjected to segregation within itself. She came to St John's from Nyasaland (now Malawi), where there was at that time no adequate provision for the segregated education of coloureds. Her conversion was the cause of considerable stress:

> My grandfather had written to the convent that he did not want his grandchildren to eat pork, and that he would pay extra money so that we could have margarine on our bread and not lard; and we did have different meals from the Christian children. He was worried about our going to church too but that was no problem for the nuns who agreed that instead we should perform domestic duties. I think one of the original reasons I wanted to go to church was to avoid those chores, and finally the nuns allowed me to, after having asked me if it was really my wish to go against my grandfather's ruling. None of my brothers and sisters went.

But through going to church Maria genuinely discovered Christianity. When he heard about her desire to convert, Hadji Osman at first wrote to the nuns forbidding them to allow her conversion, and then sent a lawyer armed with papers warning that if the nuns allowed it, he would withdraw all ten of the (fee-paying) children of his family from the school. The nuns tried to get round this by smuggling Maria to Salisbury Cathedral to be received into the Church, so that the service at least did not take place in the school chapel. It didn't save the situation. Hadji Osman withdrew all the children as soon as he heard what had happened, and that was the effective end of their education. 'I had to be cleansed from being a Christian. I had to have seven buckets of cold water poured over me, and I had to cross over seven streams, and then be dressed in white. But my father threw me out. My brothers and sisters were sent to local schools after that.'

'We were part of the system,' says Sister Aurea. 'We had to fit in. We were forced into the situation, but we did the best we could for the children who came to us. Some came via friends, some via missionaries, some via farmers who had a number of coloured children on their ranches. Some of the children had lived the African life, others hadn't.' Patson Travers says: 'I think their priority was to look after the children ... they never got involved in the segregation side of society. Nobody came to me and said, "look, you're the same as everybody else, and this school shouldn't be here." But after I'd left school, I think eventually the oneness of the human race was stressed at St John's. They were fantastic disciplinarians but they were also fantastic teachers and I could not have wished for a better start in life than having gone there.'

The system worked; and coloured school-leavers like Arthur Cubitt – who is half British, and half Portuguese-African – were typical products of it: 'Driving and welding. Those were the two jobs for us. I was in the government thirty-six years and my job was driving the posh cars. I drove the Queen, and I drove Prime Ministers like Macmillan and Wilson when they came down here. They made us coloureds drivers because whites are a bit too high up for that kind of job.' Arthur was fortunate in that his father married his mother and stood by her, and by his son: 'He never hid me behind doors because I was brown. He was a straightforward man.' He was also big and strong, and apt to knock down anyone who said anything about his marital arrangements.

Raphael Onions was born in 1928, the youngest of three sons of a white father and a black mother. His father stood by the family, but never told his own mother of their existence, keeping the secret until her death in 1955. He married his African wife formally in 1964. They had been together for more than thirty years. Jack Vlahakis' Greek father stood by all four of his local wives and had twenty-five children. But mixed marriages remained rare and mixed couples were stigmatized. As late as 1948, when the heir to the chieftaincy of the Bamangwato tribe in Bechuanaland (now Botswana), Seretse Khama, famously married a London secretary, Ruth Williams, there was uproar; in Britain, Ruth was described as a 'filthy white creature'; in South Africa, the union was seen as 'striking at the root of white supremacy'.

'Play-whites' and the Tug of War

Most mixed race people stayed in their subordinate position in society; but some were pale-skinned enough to rise above it. 'If you could conceivably play white and get away with it you would do so for the simple reason that it would guarantee you a job,' says Patson Travers:

It would also guarantee you a good area to live, and better pay. But you did it at the cost of playing hide-and-seek with society, because if the masquerade was unveiled by whites then you'd lose your position double quick. Then you'd be the mock of the coloured community when you had to move back to it, and they'd refuse to have anything to do with you. It was sad and tragic. I felt sorry for the ones whom that happened to. While they were engaged in the subterfuge, they would go out of their way to avoid being seen by a coloured person in case it was an old schoolfriend. They made friends only among the whites. One thing I noticed was that most of them never had children when they got married, and the reason for that was obvious to anyone with the slightest grasp of genetics. They were scared of having black children. Throwbacks. And of course a thing like that broke up a lot of marriages. So most of those play-whites never got married. They must have lived horrible lives.

'There were great problems if coloured children were found in white schools,' adds N. D. Atkinson, Professor of Education at Zimbabwe University. 'In the archives of the Education Department there are some very pathetic references to the predicament of parents and children who were expelled from white schools because evidence of colour was found. Even now one cannot help but feel extreme sadness at the position of children who were thus humiliated in front of their classmates.

As pressure from African nationalists grew, the whites themselves tried to court the mixed race community. In the spring of 1965, Ian Smith went to the mixed race Salisbury suburb of Arcadia on the campaign trail. 'I think one of the things I had always had in my mind was what happened in South Africa after the defeat of Smuts in 1948 – how the then Nationalist Party removed the coloured representation in the Party. I think history proved that that was a mistake because it had the effect of putting the coloureds into the opposite camp. Our philosophy generally was to bring these people along with us, to gradually incorporate them, and that was the message I was putting over to them.'

But it was too late. When Ian Smith declared UDI (the Unilateral Declaration of Independence from Great Britain) on 11 November

1965, the coloured community was torn between its loyalty to the white government it had faithfully served, and the pressure of growing demands for black rule.

Whichever side they took, their future would remain uncertain – a human product of relationships that were disapproved of by the whites and disliked by the blacks more and more as the two sides – rulers and ruled – drew apart, and as the tension between them increased. When the war of independence broke out in Rhodesia, the coloureds once more found themselves in the middle. As Patson Travers recalls, 'A lot of us didn't want to get involved – there was a belief that the war was between whites and blacks, not us. For years during the liberation war we never lost a coloured soldier, except possibly in an accident. But not in combat. The reason for that was that the leaders of the blacks believed that we were being con-scripted by the whites, and they knew that we didn't want to fight, and so orders went out not to fire on coloured brigades, not to engage in combat with them.' But as the whites left the country, more and more coloureds were encouraged to join up on the white side, and many did so, to escape unemployment. Many blacks did the same thing, for the same reason, adopting the European names which coloureds had, for the purpose. 'You knew that this guy was not a coloured, but you also knew the reason why he was prepared to go and fight was to earn a living. But once this volunteer system got into place we started losing a lot of coloured soldiers in battle, because the old rule of not engaging them couldn't apply any more.'

In the new world of liberated Africa, coloureds are still discrimi-nated against as Patson Travers explains: 'If you went to an organiz-ation which is run by blacks and they hear that your name is

Travers, or Smith or MacIntosh or whatever it might be, they know that you are part white, and if they do not know you personally, or know for sure that you were on the right side during the war, you do not get the job.' In Nyasaland, Abdul Osman had a similar experience:

> The coloured people were asked by Dr Banda whether we wanted to remain on our father's side or our mother's side. Most of us held British passports but we renounced them and said we would stay with our mother, that we would stay in Africa . . . . But we were segregated from Day One. In Malawi, there's no prominent coloured in the army, the government, the police, the civil service – nowhere. We were even denied loans to start businesses, because we weren't technically indigenous Malawians. We are aliens in our own country, and that is the bitterest thing of all.

In India, matters are not very different. Now, with the Empire gone, the Anglo-Indian is a dying type, as members of the group dilute the white genes by marrying within Indian society, and their children naturally adopt Indian language and custom. 'After Partition, the Anglo-Indian had a hard time,' says Marie Godfrey. 'We still have. The Indian is top dog. There's no doubt about it. I don't blame them.' Many left for Australia; those too poor to do so, however, had to remain behind.

But there is always hope, and though perhaps we are wrong to go on putting our trust in it, since it almost invariably disappoints, without it there would be no movement forward. Perhaps the last word should go to the Zimbabwean politician, Michael Lannas:

I do think the coloured would stay in the middle because you have to understand that in African societies you don't have half members. You're either a member or you're not a member. There may possibly be an evolutionary process like the children coming out of school today are saying: 'It's different from your time, when you went to school you were only coloured people in that school. Today we go to school together, white, black.' This might have an influence of homogenizing society, and it might possibly lead to that.

For myself, I am not angry. I just saw myself as a victimized person, born in the wrong place at the wrong time, and I realized that I had to face up to the situation and do something about it. I taught my children: you are a person. You are not a white person, you're not a black person, you're just a person, as good as anybody. You don't look up to anybody and you don't look down on anybody. This is the way you grow up.

Bibliography

Ballhatchet, Kenneth, *Race, Sex, and Class Under the Raj* (Weidenfeld & Nicolson, London, 1980).

Chaudhuri, Nupur and Strobel, Margaret (eds.), *Western Women and Imperialism – Complicity and Resistance* (Indiana UP, Indiana, 1992).

Hyam, Ronald, *Empire and Sexuality – the British Experience* (Manchester UP, Manchester, 1990).

Mason, Philip, *The Men Who Ruled India* (Jonathan Cape condensed ed., London, 1985).

Morris, James, *Heaven's Command; Pax Britannica* and *Farewell the Trumpets* (Penguin, Harmondsworth, 1979).

Index

Africa 12, 30
  colonization of, 17, 19, 24, 72, 86–7
  missionaries in, 144, 149–50
  prostitution in, 129, 141
  treatment of mixed race people in
      Zimbabwe, 173–7, 178–9, 180,
      181–2, 183
Africans 45, 115
  and Christianity, 24–5, 143
  concern over alleged child abuse by,
      116–18
  relationship with colonials, 43, 50,
      72–7, 104–6, 113–14
  segregation of, 55, 139–40
  sexuality of, 30, 34, 39, 117
alcoholism
  in army, 124
Allan, Maud 91
Amritsar
  killings at, 57–8
Anderson, Dr David 54, 112
Andrew, Elizabeth Wheeler 132
Anglo-Indians
  abuse of, 46–7
  difficulty in integration after British
      departure, 173, 182
  and East India Company, 26, 60,
      164–5
  prejudice against, 48–9, 164–7
  soldiers and, 46, 171–2
  treatment of children, 168–70
anthropology 38, 39, 41
army 20

alcoholism in, 124
avoidance of attachments with locals
    by officers, 69–71
Indians in, 71, 84–5, 124
see also soldiers
Arthur, Dr John 153–6, 158

Batten, Dr Keith 117–18
Bell, Gertrude 91
Benfield, Paul 60
Bentinck, General William 60
Besant, Annie 91
Beveridge, Annette Akroyd 91, 112
Black Hole of Calcutta 18
blacks
  sexuality of, 34–5, 39, 117
  view of superiority of whites over, 9,
      28, 38–40
  see also Africans
Boer War (1899–1902) 19
Bombay 17
  prostitution in, 126–8, 134
books
  portrayal of eroticism in, 34–5
  written on Empire, 27–9
Bowen, Harry 137
Brennan, Maria 176–7
British Empire 9–10, 161
  criticism of, 20
  growth of, 17–21
  influence on British, 9
  mixture of races in, 161
  origins, 16

population, 20–1, 123
success of, 20
Brodrick, Sir John 63
Brooks, Len 81–2
brothels 121–2, 126–7, 134
regulation of, 129–30, 131–2, 135
Bryan, Florry 96
Buganda, Kingdom of 149–50
Bundu dancers 33
Burdett-Coutts, Angela 91
Burma 65
Burton, Richard 38–9, 40, 41, 145–6
Bushnell, Dr Kate 132
Butler, Josephine 131

Cabot, John 16
Calcutta 17, 18, 22, 89, 90
Canada 16
Cape, the 19
Casement, Sir Roger 42
Charnock, Job 62
Chatterjee, Dr Ratnabali 62–3, 78, 79, 136, 144
Chege, Jane 151, 152, 154–5, 156
Cheptothon, Mary 43–4
children
concern over alleged African abuse of, 116–18
segregation of mixed race people in Zimbabwe, 173–7
treatment of Anglo-Indian, 168–70
Chisholm, Caroline 91
Christianity
and the Africans, 24–5, 143
imposing of on native cultures, 144–5, 159–60
pressure on mixed race people to convert to, 162, 176–7
and sexual morality, 145–8, 150
Church of Scotland Mission 153–5,
158
circumcision, female 150–2, 153–60
Clive, Robert 18
Collins, Brigadier Tom 83–4, 103
colonials 23, 121
abuse of power, 57–8
and administration of Empire, 20, 57
attractions of working in the Empire, 26, 29
desire for sexual aloofness, 30, 31, 64, 68, 77, 123
disadvantages encountered, 21–3, 66–7
and imposing of Christianity on locals, 24–5, 144–5, 159–60
lack of interest in native cultures, 23–5
and mixed marriages, 65–6, 67, 70–1, 96, 179
prejudice against Anglo-Indians, 48–9, 164–7, 168–70
recruitment and training of, 59–60, 63
relationship with Africans, 43, 50, 72–7, 105–6, 113–14
segregation from locals, 26–7, 51, 55, 60–1, 80, 139–41
sexual relations with locals, 30, 31, 32–4, 37, 42–6, 67–8, 71, 78–9
see also prostitution
treatment of mixed race people in Zimbabwe, 162–3, 173–7, 178–9, 180, 181–2, 183
view of own superiority, 9, 28, 38–40
women as see women
writings of, 27–9
see also army; soldiers
Contagious Diseases Acts (1866) 131, 132

Cornwallis, Governor-General 26, 60, 164

Cousins, Margaret 91

Crewe Circular (1909–34) 68, 73, 74

Cubitt, Arthur 178

Curzon, Lord 63–4, 96–8, 128

Dadet, Helen 150, 158–9, 160

dancers
Bundu, 33
nautch, 35–7, 144

Dasi, Taramoni 118

Daula, Suraj-al 18

death penalty 116–17

Disraeli, Benjamin 15–16

District Officers 20, 57, 63

Dubey, Colonel Guyan 104

Dubey, Major-General Uday 71–2

Duncan, Governor John 60

Dyer, Alfred 127–8, 131, 132

Dyer, Brigadier-General Reginald 57–8

East India College (Haileybury) 59

East India Company 17–18
Anglo-Indians in, 26, 60, 164–5, 164–5
officials of, 61–2
and public administration, 18, 24, 60
recruitment, 59–60

education
segregation of in Zimbabwe, 163, 175–8

Elliot, Jane 105, 114, 115

Empire and Sexuality (Hyam) 31, 146–7

Epstein, Fanny 127

Fanshawe, Henrietta 72–3, 104, 106

films

concern over portrayal of women in, 94–5
portrayal of eroticism, 34–5

Fraser, William 62

Frith, Tony 32–3, 44–5

Gavaghan, Terence 73–7

George V, King 20, 89

Gillies, Josiah Dashwood 165

Glyn, Elinor 64

Godfrey, Marie 168–70, 170–1, 182

Graham, John Anderson 168–9

Grogan, Ewart 86–7, 113–15, 116

Hamilton, Lord 97–8

Hastie, Rev. William 166–7

homosexuality 31, 42, 98, 123, 125

Hooper, Cyril 151, 153

Hooper, Elizabeth 152

Hübner, Baron von 92

Hughes, Captain W. A. C. 85–6

Hume, Mrs James 112

Hunt, James 39

Ilbert Bill (1883) 111–12

India 11, 16, 30, 66, 72
administration in, 57, 89–90, 111–12
see also East India Company
colonization of, 17–18, 23–4
cultural effect of British intervention in, 79
departure of British from, 173
missionaries in, 144
prostitution in, 37, 121–2, 126–8, 129–30, 131, 134–5, 136
Queen Victoria becomes Empress of, 15–16, 31

Indian Mutiny (1857) 31, 84, 93, 108–11, 165

Indians
  in army, 71, 84–5, 124
  dancers, 33–4, 35–7, 144
  as mistresses of British officials,
    62–3, 78
  relationship with colonials, 48–51,
    78–9, 80, 96–7
  segregation of, 26–7, 60–1, 51, 80
  sexuality of, 30, 31, 37
  view of by white women, 97–8
  see also Anglo-Indians

Jones, Sir William 28

Kanpur 137
  massacre at, 109–10, 111
Karpurthala, Rajah of 97
Kenya
  female circumcision in, 150–2,
    153–60
Khama, Seretse 179
Kikuyu tribe
  and female circumcision, 150–2,
    153–6, 158
  working on white farms, 113
Kingsley, Mary 27

Lannas, Michael 182–3
Livingstone, David 24–5, 148
'lock hospitals' 130–1
Lucknow siege 109, 110, 111
Lustful Turk, The 34–5

Macdonald, Sir Hector 41–2
MacFarlane, Iris 40, 48–9, 50, 102–3,
    162
McKenna, Donal 121–2, 133–4
Madras 17
marriage
  in the army, 79–80, 122, 124

polygyny, 145–6, 153
  view of mixed, 65–6, 67, 70–1, 96,
    179
Mason, Philip 57
Matthews, Betty 106–8
Mau Mau uprising (1952–7) 87
Mayne, Rupert 83, 172
Mehta, Hurroo 112
Metcalfe, Charles 61
Military Cantonments Act (1889) 131,
    132
Milner, Sir Alfred 63–4
missionaries 143–4
  clashes over female circumcision in
    Kenya, 150–2, 153–60
  in Kingdom of Buganda 149–50
  Moslems as, 149
  preachers of sexual morality, 146–8,
    150, 153
  prejudice within, 165–7
  success of, 144
mixed races 162
  and Christianity, 162, 176–7
  employment, 162
  segregation of in Zimbabwe, 162–3,
    173–7, 178–9, 180, 181–2, 183
  treatment of children, 168–70,
    173–4
  see also Anglo-Indians
Moral Guardian 123
Moslems 149
Muciiri, Kibe 87
Mullan, Kit 49–50, 55, 99–100, 105–6,
    144
Munro, Sir Thomas 20
Mwanga (ruler of Buganda) 149–50

Nairobi 113
Nasoor, Marion 42
nautch dancers 35–7, 144

Nell, Dr 64–5
Nevill, Pran 37
Ngumba, Ben 153–4, 155
Norris, Mrs J. F. 111–12

Onions, Raphael 178–9
Osman, Abdul 176, 182
Osman, Hadji 176–7

Patiala, Maharajah of 96
Pierce, Edna 46–7, 172–3
pig-sticking 80
Pigot, Mary 166–7
Plassey, battle of 18
polygyny 145–6, 153
Portuguese 17
prostitution 33
    in Africa, 129, 141
    attempts to control venereal disease,
        130–2
    Europeans as, 126–8
    increase in, 126
    in India, 37, 121–2, 126–8, 129–30,
        131, 134–5, 136
    and Purity movements, 123, 127–8
    regulation of brothels, 129–30,
        131–2, 135
Pryke, Colonel Wallace 69–70, 79, 80,
    81, 103–4, 136–7
Pumwani (African shanty town)
    140–1
Purity movements 123, 127–8, 131–2

rape
    and death penalty, 117–18
    by soldiers on local women, 118–20
    and tightening of laws on, 140
Residents 61–2
Rhodesia see Zimbabwe
Roe, Sir Thomas 17

Sahib, Nana 109
salt protest (1930) 118
Sarkies, Dr John 85, 122, 135
scandals, sex 41–2, 125
Schreiner, Olive 28
Sellon, Edward 37, 38
sex 10
    age of consent, 30–1
    anthropology and, 38–40
    in colonies, 30, 31, 32–4, 37, 42–6,
        67–8, 71, 78–9
        see also prostitution
    and Crewe Circular, 68, 73, 74
    homosexuality, 31, 42, 98, 123, 125
    preaching of sexual morality by
        missionaries, 146–8, 150, 153
    Purity movements and, 123, 127–8,
        131–2
    repression of in Victorian era,
        29–30, 31–2, 42, 66, 135
    scandals associated with, 41–2, 125
    and segregation, 139–41
    sexual assault against Europeans,
        117–18
    soldiers and, 81, 121–2, 123–4, 129,
        136–9
    view of African sexuality, 34, 39,
        117
        see also venereal disease
Shahjehan 17
Sharma, Lieutenant-Colonel Gautam
    84, 124, 126–7
Sharp, Martin 50–4
Shaw, Flora 28
Shebbeare, Frances 98–9
Sheldon, May French 27
Silberrad, Hubert 67–8
Simla 99
Singh, Yardonath 119
Skinner, James 62, 164

Smith, Ian 173–4, 175, 180–1
soldiers
    and Anglo-Indian women, 46, 171–2
    local women's fear of, 119–20
    and marriage, 79–80, 122, 124
    and sex, 81, 121–2, 123–4, 129,
        136–7
    social life, 136–8
    sport taken up, 80–1
    and venereal disease, 122, 129, 130,
        133, 134, 135, 137
    see also army
Soles, Ethel 152, 155–6
St John's Convent (Harare) 175–6,
    178
Stanton-Ife, Douglas 68–9, 77, 171–2
Stead, W. T. 128
Steel, Dorothy 100–2
Stephenson, J. E 'Chirupula' 65–6
Stumpf, Hulda 157–8

Temple, Merfyn 147–8, 156–7,
    159–60
'300 Club' 83
Thug cult 60
Travers, Patson 162–3, 174, 175–6,
    179–80, 181–2
Trevelyan, C. E. 124, 165

Ulyate, Mrs 117–18

venereal disease (VD) 33, 118
    Africans and, 55, 117
    attempts to control, 130–2
    failure to eradicate, 139
    soldiers and, 122, 129, 130, 133, 134,
        135, 137
    treatment of, 133
Victoria, Queen 15–16, 31

Walters, Captain 64–5
Wambui, Atta 154, 156
Wellesley, Marquess Richard 61
'white slavery' 127–8
Wiarimu, Margaret 76, 141
Williams, Ruth 179
Wintel, Sister Aurea 176, 178
women, British
    life in colonies, 21–2, 60, 61, 99–100
    and opposition to Ilbert Bill, 111–12
    relationships with locals, 48–50
    role of, 92–3, 103–4
    seen to be in peril, 35, 94–5, 105–6,
        111, 116, 118
    stereotype of, 93–4
    working in the Empire, 90–1
    writings of, 27

Zimbabwe
    segregation of mixed race people in,
        162–3, 173–7, 178–9, 180,
        181–2, 183